I0819152

Praise for Lift Your Eyes

Pastor Joshua Pfeiffer echoes Luther's insistence that Christian life is not self-enclosed; it is a life lived outside of the self through faith in Christ and through love in service to the neighbor. The Christian lives with feet firmly planted in creation but with eyes fixed on the hope that is ours because Jesus is Lord over death. Pastor Pfeiffer demonstrates how our faith and the hope that it brings does not evacuate Christians from the world but enlivens believers for their callings in creation.

—John T. Pless, assistant professor of pastoral ministry and mission, Concordia Theological Seminary, Fort Wayne, Indiana

---

Lift Your Eyes is a much-needed pastoral guide for Christians shaped by a culture that urges constant self-focus. Joshua Pfeiffer redirects our gaze upward to Christ and outward to those around us, drawing deeply from Scripture and Luther's theology. This is not a self-improvement book offering empty promises but an invitation to true rest in Christ's righteousness—freeing you to love others in ways that truly count.

—Marcus "FLAME" Gray, GRAMMY®-nominated and Stellar Award–winning hip hop artist; author of Extra Nos: Discovering Grace Outside Myself *and* Because Jesus Taught It: Christianity Through the Eyes of the Church Fathers

---

This book heralds the arrival of a gifted new writer with a warm heart and a popular touch. In this book, Joshua Pfeiffer tackles some of the darkest, deepest issues in our self-absorbed society in a lucid, winsome way. He weaves a colorful tapestry of biblical, personal, practical, and pastoral insights into a bright, coherent vision of life in the world. With the eyes of a skilled artist, he explores various kinds of looking—*away* from ourselves, *up* to Jesus in faith and thanksgiving, and *out* to others in love, so that we can look honestly *into* ourselves and *forward* in hope to eternal life with God.

—Dr. John W. Kleinig

The strength of *Lift Your Eyes* lies in its call to look outside ourselves. Instead of navel-gazing and disputing with neighbors (Christian or not), our focus can be drawn up to God in faith and out to others in love. This book would be beneficial for laypeople as they consider their stance before the world as servants, not rulers.

—Jessica Bordeleau, MAR; theological media producer,
Concordia Seminary, St. Louis, Missouri

LIFT YOUR EYES

How to Live Outside Yourself

JOSHUA PFEIFFER

CONCORDIA PUBLISHING HOUSE · SAINT LOUIS

TO KIMBERLEY

Published by Concordia Publishing House
3558 S. Jefferson Ave., St. Louis, MO 63118-3968
1-800-325-3040 • cph.org

Manufactured in the United States of America

1 2 3 4 5 6 7 8 9 10 35 34 33 32 31 30 29 28 27 26

We conclude, therefore, that a Christian lives not in himself, but in Christ and in his neighbor. Otherwise he is not a Christian. He lives in Christ through faith, in his neighbor through love. By faith he is caught up beyond himself into God. By love he descends beneath himself into his neighbor.

MARTIN LUTHER
(*LUTHER'S WORKS*, VOL. 31, P. 371)

CONTENTS

Foreword . . . 7
Introduction . . . 11

PART 1: Cultural and Theological Foundations

1. Looking In: The Problem . . . 21
2. Looking Up and Looking Out: The Dynamic . . . 37

PART 2: Christian Living as Lifting Our Eyes

3. Looking Up in Faith: The Heart and Center . . . 57
4. Looking Up in Thanksgiving: The Joyful Response . . . 73
5. Looking Out in Brotherly Love: The Christian Community . . . 89
6. Looking Out in Neighborly Love: Service in the World . . . 105
7. Looking In Rightly: The Daily Death of the Old Self . . . 121
8. Looking Forward in Hope: The Anticipation . . . 137

Conclusion . . . 155
Scripture Index . . . 161

FOREWORD

The direction of our gaze at our own lives and at our involvement in the world around us often turns inward. Martin Luther described those born without trust in their Creator as "turned in upon themselves" (*incurvatus in se*). This navel-gazing results in stumbling over the lives of others, slipping on the ice of a frozen world, or crashing into the walls that God has set in place to protect us from wandering from life as He designed it. Wrapping ourselves into a ball to protect ourselves or to find warmth in a frigid world cripples us. Tied up in ourselves, we grow stiff and lose the ability to move freely in the way God made us to as we care for His creatures.

In this book, Pastor Joshua Pfeiffer sounds the Holy Scriptures' call to those turned in on themselves, to those turned away from their Creator and the creatures to whom He has connected them in various communities. This call summons us out of ourselves and gives us the gift of relaxing in the presence of our Lord. It summons us out of being all knotted up in ourselves, entangled in the shreds into which we tear our own lives. For, as Paul explained to the Romans, Jesus Christ has placed our sins in His grave and died under their weight. He has restored our righteousness, our identity as children of God, through His resurrection (Romans 4:25; 6:1–13; cf. Colossians 2–3). Through His incarnation, the Second Person of the Holy Trinity has eradicated the identity of His people as sinners living in doubt and defiance over against God and His Word. He has taken our sins and sealed them in His tomb. He has raised us up to walk in His footsteps in self-sacrificial obedience to God's command to be His light and His salt among His human creatures and in His created universe.

God is deeply engaged in conversation with His human creatures, ever since He went looking for us and called out to Adam, "Where are you?" (Genesis 3:9). God could not abide not being present in the lives of His human creatures. He came into human skin and bones as the Word made flesh and promised to abide with us into eternity. He has created community with us through His call to return to His family. He invites us to join Him at His Supper Table in the company of the others in the family from throughout the world. He wants us to stop singing, "I did it my way," and do it His way. He wants us to practice singing, "Glory to God and to the Lamb," already in the little acts of kindness and gentleness that convey His love in the midst of life as we experience it day in and day out. For this is His way—the only way, in fact—to enjoy His gift of life.

Pfeiffer guides readers to the fullness of blessing that comes from having life opened up to embrace our Creator and His world instead of wrapping our arms around ourselves. He points us to the biblical picture of life, which focuses on God and His expression of love for us. This is a way of life that takes seriously God's observation that it is not good for us to be alone (Genesis 2:18). It is a way of life that envisions true human joy and peace in being open to loving and serving Him by loving and serving other human beings in the self-sacrificial way that Jesus has modeled for us. Pfeiffer stimulates readers to open their eyes to the full horizons that God has set for His human creatures as He placed Adam and Eve together as the founders of human community. The author's insightful exposition of Scripture opens readers' eyes to perceive more fully what it means that God has given us back our identity as His creatures and children after we had thrown it away by sinfully seeking to find our identity, and the security and meaning it gives, in persons or things that He has created.

As the basis of his exploration of the godly way of life that brings us the blessings God intends for us, Pfeiffer lays out the definition of being human that Martin Luther discovered in Scripture. The Wittenberg reformer affirmed in the preface to his Galatians lectures of 1531, published in 1535, that "our theology" *is* the distinction of our passive righteousness as the reborn children of God from our active righteousness, which consists of our thoughts, words, and deeds as His godly children. This anthropology—in Luther's own words, "our theology"—distinguishes our core identity, given by God when His re-creative Word of promise re-creates us as His reborn children, from our actions that match that new identity. We receive this core identity passively, as a gift; our secondary identities express themselves in our active thoughts, words, and deeds. Pfeiffer uses this definition of what it means to be our Creator's human creatures to encourage and empower readers to live according to God's plan for human life on the basis of their confidence in God's promise of new life in and through our Lord and Savior, Jesus Christ.

In his conversation with readers in this book, Pastor Pfeiffer leads us to think in the ways the biblical writers thought about living the God-pleasing life that brings life to its fullest, with the peace and joy that only Christ's promise of new life under the guidance of the Holy Spirit bestows. This is a book to read a couple of times and come back to a few months later, for it refreshes and redirects our lives into the way of peace. It enlivens and stimulates our appreciation for God's gifts in daily life and our love for this Creator, who does not leave us or forsake us. *Lift Your Eyes* offers a feast to savor, a spread to chew on for a long time.

Robert Kolb

Lutherstadt Wittenberg, August 18, 2025

INTRODUCTION

[We] look for the resurrection of the dead and the life of the world to come.

The Nicene Creed

In the creeds of the church, Christians say what we believe. We believe in God the Father. We believe in Jesus Christ, His Son. We believe in the Holy Spirit. It has always struck me, however, that toward the end of the Nicene Creed, another verb appears seemingly out of nowhere. It has to do with the resurrection of the dead and the life of the world to come. We say that we *look* for these things. Of course, we also *believe* these truths; in fact, one might say this looking is simply faith turned toward the future or that looking presupposes faith. Whatever the case, there is this different word. Why is that? What does it mean to *look* for resurrection and a coming new life? The church here, through her creeds, encourages us to adopt something like a spiritual posture in the world that can be described as looking in anticipation. Looking is a metaphor for the orientation we have in our whole lives as Christian people, although there is a literal sense here

We *believe* in the resurrection and the life of the world to come, but we also *look* for them.

as well. We are to live as people who are spiritually alert and waiting in expectation for God's promised full redemption. Yes, we *believe* in the resurrection and the life of the world to come, but we also *look* for them.

The attentive Bible reader may notice a certain tension here. After all, Paul famously reminds us that "we walk by faith, not by sight" (2 Corinthians 5:7) and that "faith comes from hearing, and hearing through the word of Christ" (Romans 10:17). John says, "Blessed are those who have not seen and yet have believed" (John 20:29). Even Luther was fond of speaking of the ear as the organ of faith. Often in life, we cannot see what God is doing or why He is allowing certain things to happen. As such, we are to trust not what we see with human eyes but rather what God promises us in His Word.

Even so, the authors of Scripture offer us various images of the Christian life. In addition to the need for the literal hearing of God's Word in order to live by faith, we also learn of a spiritual posture that can be described as a type of looking. Paul himself, having emphasized the hearing aspect of faith, speaks somewhat paradoxically of looking to what is unseen as a dimension of our faith (2 Corinthians 4:18) and of "the eyes of [our] hearts" being enlightened (Ephesians 1:18). The author to the Hebrews describes the whole Christian life as a race of perseverance in which we are always "looking to Jesus, the founder and perfecter of our faith" (Hebrews 12:2). Jesus encourages His disciples to lift up their eyes and look around at the fields ripe for harvest (John 4:35), and His parables testify that His disciples should be alert and keeping watch for His return (Matthew 24:42–44). Hearing God's Word in faith is indeed crucial. Yet the Scriptures also present to us a theme of *looking* in faith.

In this book, I use this spiritual posture of looking to explore the Christian life in the context of today's world. While there are powerful forces at work encouraging us to look inward for hope, identity, purpose, and meaning—indeed, for life itself—Christians are fundamentally to look elsewhere, to lift our eyes from ourselves. We look *up* to God in faith, and we look *out* to our neighbor in love. Martin Luther was insistent on this point. God and neighbor. Faith and love. Looking up and looking out. When we get that right, we do truly look forward in joyful anticipation to the resurrection of the dead and the life of the world to come, and there is even a sense in which we can rightly look in at ourselves.

The Scriptures also present to us a theme of *looking* in faith.

The following chapters explore the dynamics of the Christian life using this spirituality of looking, as well as how it interacts with literal activities of looking in our lives. This book will especially take into consideration the contemporary cultural context of the Western world and will draw deeply on the Bible and Luther's theology. However, I'm confident that Christians from all traditions will resonate with many of the insights offered here.

The book is in two parts. In part 1 (chapters 1–2), I offer brief cultural analyses and theological foundations to set the stage for the rest of the book. In part 2, I unpack the biblical foundations and theological insights in detail and present a practical application for the Christian life.

In chapter 1, I explore a trend identified by a number of authors that is sometimes referred to as expressive individualism. This way of understanding the world and our lives pervades both the wider culture and the church. It is complex and multifaceted, as most things are in life, but something of its essence is captured by the phrase "looking in."

In chapter 2, I begin to offer the alternative vision for life that God reveals to us, articulated especially using Lutheran theology. We live in two realms—before God and before the neighbor. To be rightly related in those two realms is to be in a twofold state of righteousness. This means there are primarily two different ways to inhabit these realms—by faith and by love. This is the two-dimensional vision of what it is to be truly human.

Chapter 3 begins part 2 of the book. I go to the heart and center of this life—namely, the passive righteousness of Christ we receive from God by faith and in Baptism. This righteousness grants us a new identity as children of God. Here is the primary contrast between the Christian and the expressive individualist: Christians don't begin by looking in at ourselves; rather, we look up to God and His grace in Christ. This is an ongoing dimension of our life as we lift our eyes in faith to God's promises in His Word and in the Lord's Supper.

In chapter 4, I consider our initial response to God's grace in Christ—a second dimension of looking up to God, but now in thanksgiving, prayer, and praise. The modern person often lives with a sense of gratitude, but where or to whom is it directed? Christians live by looking up to God for grace and then by looking up to Him in thanksgiving for that grace.

In chapter 5, I move to another aspect of our response to God's action for us—looking out to others in love. We first consider especially our relationships with fellow brothers and sisters in Christ and the implications this response has for Christian community. The same God who restores us to Himself places us in a family with brothers and sisters. This is the life of the church. In an individualistic age, the authentic communal life within the local congregation can be a powerful witness.

In chapter 6, I cast a wider vision of looking out, lifting our eyes to consider how we serve our neighbor more generally. This is the primary place for a Christian's good works. The Christian is freed from having to earn God's favor because of the gift of righteousness. As such, we are free to serve in the vocations in which God places us. In a time when many people are disoriented as to their direction in life, the life of loving service in vocation can provide concrete and practical guidance.

In chapter 7, I return to the theme of looking in. Initially, this was our main problem, but now I explore how there can be a proper way of looking in. There is an active putting to death of the old, sinful self and a striving for holiness that require self-examination. Once we know that we primarily look up to God in faith to find peace and security, we can rightly look in without fear.

In chapter 8, I return to the opening words of this introduction, that having oriented our lives around looking up to God and out to neighbor, we also look forward in hope to the resurrection of the dead and the life of the world to come. This is an active but patient looking in anticipation, as we do not know when Jesus will return.

This is life as it was meant to be in Eden—harmoniously related to both the Creator and His creation rather than turned in on ourselves.

It's not only that this way of life—lifting our eyes to look up and out, rather than in—is what God teaches us to do, and so we obey. It's also that this is good for us. Orienting our lives this way brings true freedom, peace, and joy. This is life as it was meant to be in Eden—harmoniously related to both the Creator and His creation rather than turned in on ourselves. In this fallen world, our looking up and out will continue to be marred by sin. But a life so oriented is the life God intends for our flourishing, and even in this broken world, this life is the beginning of God's great renewal of all things.

PART 1

Cultural and Theological Foundations

CHAPTER 1

LOOKING IN

The Problem

The heart is deceitful above
all things, and desperately sick;
who can understand it?
JEREMIAH 17:9

LOOKING IN

A father and his young adult daughter sat down to talk. His daughter tried to express what she was going through: "I'm so confused about who I am and where I'm going in life. When I was a child, life seemed simpler. Now my friendships seem to come and go. The dreams I had for my career haven't been working out the way I had hoped. I look inside and ask myself who I really am, but I'm not so sure anymore. I search my heart to try and discover what my passions are and where I should go next in life, but there, too, it all feels hazy and uncertain."

The father listened, noting her pain and confusion. He loved her dearly. Yet he was struck by how much she had been influenced by a trend he had noticed in many places: the tendency to look *inside* for a sense of identity, purpose, and meaning in life. As a Christian father, he slowly and gently considered how he might encourage her to lift her eyes from herself to the God who created, redeemed, and sanctified her, to where God had placed her in life to serve others. It would seemingly be a long journey.

The Christian faith has always offered clear and, for many people, compelling answers to life's big questions. For the person asking about his or her identity, a Christian response might point them to their creation in the image of God, to their status as a child of God through their Baptism into Christ, to their being part of the Body of Christ in the life of the church, or to their being a person in whom the Holy Spirit dwells. For someone asking about their purpose in life, a Christian reply might direct them toward humanity's role as stewards of creation, to the central reality of knowing God through His Son, Jesus Christ, or to the call to love one's neighbor. Within a Christian framework, these big questions can be answered in varying ways with different accents and emphases, but the main point is that there have always been answers to give. And because Christianity served as a foundation for much of Western culture, many people in the past felt a sense of stability.

Within a Christian framework, these big questions can be answered.

Now, however, that stability is challenged in various ways. One way is by simply seeking alternative answers to the ones traditionally given by Christianity. People have increasingly turned to other religions, spiritualities, philosophies, and worldviews to find answers to questions of identity, purpose, and meaning. A more radical way is by giving up on the questions themselves. This approach suggests that trying to find a stable identity and a reason for being is naive because this world and our lives in it are simply the result of unguided, random chance.

But there is another, more common impulse in Western culture today that challenges the Christian faith and our sense of stability. Most people do continue to search for deeper truth and do desire to live what they consider to be good lives, but rather than looking to Christianity or any other external source, they look inside themselves to find answers. From a Christian perspective, this is a problem, and it's this problem I seek to respond to in this book.

EXPRESSIVE INDIVIDUALISM

A number of people in recent decades have noticed and talked about this trend. One phrase that captures much of what I have in mind is "expressive individualism." First coined by Robert Bellah and his fellow sociologists as they studied American culture, the phrase was picked up by Canadian philosopher Charles Taylor to describe what he noticed in contemporary life. Most recently, Carl Trueman has built on this work in pointing out how the trend has manifested in an even more powerful way in connection with movements linked to the sexual revolution. So, how do these authors describe this thing called expressive individualism?

It has been Taylor, in his widely acclaimed book *A Secular Age*, who has most helpfully investigated both the historical roots of expressive individualism and what it looks like in our culture today. Before we get to the specifically "expressivist" part, let's briefly explore what Taylor has to say about individualism more generally.

Taylor's book is mainly about how the Western world has changed over the last fifteen hundred years and why it was once basically inconceivable not to believe in God, whereas now, it's not only conceivable but perhaps the default position. His arguments are incredibly detailed and complex, but overall, he identifies five major shifts that have led to our secular age. The first two shifts hold the most relevance for our discussion. First is the shift from an enchanted world, in which everything is charged with spiritual power or sacred meaning, to a disenchanted world. This also involved a change in how people see themselves, from "porous" to "buffered" selves—that is, from people who can be influenced by outside spiritual forces to those who are shielded from these. The second major shift is toward a more individualistic approach to life, and interestingly, Taylor links these two shifts together.

As he summarizes the reality of disenchantment, Taylor writes, "This involved the growth and entrenchment of a new self-understanding of our social existence, one which gave an unprecedented primacy to the individual."[1] In the age of enchantment, not only was the world charged with the sacred, but society itself was understood as being embedded in a sacred order. Community members understood themselves to interact with a transcendent realm through communal ritual. This perspective changed with disenchantment: The self became buffered not only from spiritual forces in the world but from other selves as well, which created a sense of private space that further fragmented social relations. In other words, according to Taylor, this trend toward individualism started a long time ago.

1 Charles Taylor, *A Secular Age* (The Belknap Press of Harvard University Press, 2007), 146.

Let me offer an illustration to show the depth of this problem. In my garden, there are sometimes weeds that have taken root in a relatively shallow way and so are easy to remove. Occasionally, though, what I think will be a bit of quick weeding becomes a backyard battle that gets more difficult the more I get into it. What I had thought was a simple, small weed is actually the outgrowth of an underground system of roots that spreads right across the yard and goes deeper than I had anticipated. In this case, rather than quickly pulling out a single weed and thinking I've attended to the issue, it's worth taking a step back to consider the bigger picture and the actual depth of the problem. The trend of expressive individualism is like this. It's not a shallow weed, an aberration that we can expect to pull out easily. It has deep roots and requires thoughtful responses.

The trend of expressive individualism . . . has deep roots and requires thoughtful responses.

While some trace individualism back to the Enlightenment in the 1600s and 1700s, Taylor would say it simply took on a particular form during the Enlightenment—namely, with a focus on reason and what he calls instrumental control. However, there were also movements that reacted strongly against this emphasis on reason, such as Romanticism, which emphasized art, creativity, emotion, and subjectivity. This, too, was individualistic in many ways. In that stream, Taylor finds the roots of the specifically *expressive* form of individualism. From that Romantic period in the 1800s, we can fast-forward to the 1960s, where we'll find a consumerist culture after World War II and a people increasingly encouraged to express their own preferences and tastes. The next step is that this sense of individual self-expression comes to be seen not only as an important part of life but as the defining characteristic of each person's life.

NEW SENSE OF SELF

Taylor summarizes how expressive individualism has resulted in a whole new understanding of being human, in which people look inward for identity, purpose, and meaning. In a discussion of what Taylor calls the Age of Authenticity, he offers something of a definition of expressive individualism:

> **That each one of us has his/her own way of realizing our humanity, and that it is important to find and live out one's own, as against surrendering conformity with a model imposed on us from outside, by society, or the previous generation, or religious or political authority.**[2]

Notice first the use of the word *outside*. The major contrast here is between receiving something from outside oneself and cultivating something from inside. That outside reality could be a human community of some kind—hence, individualism—or another authority, including the church or even God Himself. Second, note the reference to this individualism as a way of realizing our very humanity. This is what makes expressive individualism so radical and such a challenge to Christianity. This outlook is deeper than wanting an opportunity to express one's personal

Self-expression becomes the way we determine a fuller sense of who we are and our very purpose in life.

2 Taylor, *Secular Age*, 475.

preferences—self-expression becomes the way we determine a fuller sense of who we are and our very purpose in life.

Taylor also speaks specifically about the influence of expressive individualism on religion and spirituality. In a discussion of the era when people began to choose their own Christian denomination rather than simply belonging to the one associated with wherever they lived, Taylor writes:

> **But the expressivist outlook takes this a stage farther. The religious life or practice that I become part of must not only be my choice, but it must speak to me, it must make sense in terms of my spiritual development as I understand this. This takes us farther. . . . If the focus is going now to be on my spiritual path, thus on what insights come to me in the subtler languages that I find meaningful, then maintaining this or any other framework becomes increasingly difficult.**[3]

Expressive individualism is not only something that is happening in the culture outside the church, but it is well and truly a trend *within* the church and that Christians have absorbed to one degree or another. This is why expressive individualism matters for this book. Let me offer another illustration.

The area where I currently live is prone to bushfires. Nearby national parks full of trees and bushland provide ample fuel for a fire after a lightning strike. If the winds pick up, it can be a dangerous situation. As firefighters battle these fires and the winds swirl and sometimes change direction, it can be difficult to know on which front to focus their attention. Then there is the phenomenon of spot fires. This happens when a team is

3 Taylor, *Secular Age*, 486.

working to contain the fire on one front, and the wind takes embers and starts a fire somewhere behind the team. These spot fires have been known to start up a surprisingly long distance beyond where containment teams are working. With their focus on the fire raging in front of them, it can be hard for firefighters to see that this same fire has flared up behind their backs, within their own area of safety. So it goes with cultural trends and the church. If our focus is only on how expressive individualism manifests "out there," apart from the Christian community, we may miss seeing what is happening within our own circles—and even within our own souls.

Taylor goes on to make many other interesting and helpful observations about how this trend appears in our culture. One of these is that the rise of expressive individualism has often been closely connected to questions of sexual fulfillment. A second is a rise in psychological therapy. Taylor notes that "therapies multiply which promise to help find yourself, realize yourself, release yourself, and so on."[4] These cultural insights have been picked up and developed by Carl Trueman in his book *The Rise and Triumph of the Modern Self*.[5] Trueman argues that this trajectory of expressive individualism has manifested in an even more profound way in the contemporary transgender movement. Thus, if a man or woman feels they are trapped in the opposite biological body, expressive individualism requires that their "true self" be expressed and subsequently recognized by society at large. When we ask our big and most basic life

4 Taylor, *Secular Age*, 475.

5 Carl R. Trueman, *The Rise and Triumph of the Modern Self: Cultural Amnesia, Expressive Individualism, and the Road to the Sexual Revolution* (Crossway, 2020).

questions—Who am I? Where am I going in life?—the answer in Western culture today has become "Let me look inside myself and tell you."

INTROSPECTION

So, what do Christians make of all this? How might the Christian father in our opening story begin to think this through and speak to his beloved daughter? We can acknowledge that there has always been an introspective dimension of what it means to be human. I recall a discussion about the differences between animals and humans, and the topic of thinking came up. "Dogs and cats can think too," person A said. "Yes," person B replied, "but human beings can *think* about their thoughts." Person A smiled, recognizing this simple but profound difference.

Turning to the Bible, we might think of Mary, who is recorded by Luke as "pondering . . . in her heart" the events around the birth of Jesus (Luke 2:19). The Psalms, too, composed by God's people of old, reveal versions of this inner life. For example, we read, "How long must I take counsel in my soul and have sorrow in my heart all the day?" (Psalm 13:2), and "Why are you cast down, O my soul, and why are you in turmoil within me?" (Psalm 42:5a). Here, too, there is a sense of looking in. Looking in is not the problem. The problem is why you're looking in and whether any other source of truth is allowed to be part of the conversation. The psalmists never look in and take counsel in themselves to find the final answers to life's big questions. In fact, in the second verse quoted above, the psalmist goes on

God's people live in the awareness that they are always in His presence, even if they quietly take counsel within.

to say to his own soul, "Hope in God; for I shall again praise Him, my salvation and my God" (Psalm 42:5b–6). Looking in does not exclude God. Rather, God's people live in the awareness that they are always in His presence, even if they quietly take counsel within.

While introspection is a privilege of being human, there is a shadow side to this dynamic.

THE DECEPTIVE HEART

At the beginning of this chapter, I quoted the prophet Jeremiah: "The heart is deceitful above all things, and desperately sick; who can understand it?" (Jeremiah 17:9). As fallen people this side of Eden, our inner life can be messy and confusing, to say the least. In fact, we cannot even truly understand the inner workings of our own minds and hearts. Even more than this, Jeremiah says our own hearts can deceive us! We all know this happens. If, in our sinful desires, we really want to do something, we can convince ourselves in very clever and devious ways that it is the right thing to do. Interestingly, the Lutheran Confessions also use this verse to explain why our consciences should not be burdened to name every sin before we receive absolution. Our hearts are so deceitful, sick, and impossible to understand that we can't even sort out the problem, let alone the solution. Jeremiah warns of all sorts of difficulties when we look inside ourselves to find truth.

Here's an example that often comes up as I work through the Ten Commandments with young Christians. Think about the Eighth Commandment, which forbids false testimony and lying. Have you ever had the experience of telling a story to a family member or friend and recounting the event in a way that puts yourself in a better light? Perhaps a little voice reminds you in your conscience that this is not the way it actually happened. Yet, on the story goes in the version we prefer. The next step is the more serious one—when we forget the fabrication and start to believe our version of the story is reality. This is the deceptiveness of the human heart at work. Almost every person I have ever talked to about this sort of experience knows exactly what I am getting at.

Another famous biblical case of introspection, of sorts, is Paul's discussion of the Law and sin in Romans 7. As he looks in, he laments, "For I do not understand my own actions. For I do not do what I want, but I do the very thing I hate" (v. 15). In the psalms quoted in the earlier section, the inner sorrow is caused by external circumstances. However, in Paul's case, his inner turmoil is in realizing that the problems also come from within. He struggles to understand how, on the one hand, there is this desire in him to do the right thing, but on the other hand, there is a competing desire to which he often succumbs. "What is going on inside of me?" Paul asks. As with the prophet Jeremiah, Paul does not think looking inside ourselves is a good way to go.

Most important, this is all consistent with what Jesus said about the human heart. In one place, Jesus spoke to the Pharisees and scribes about their human traditions regarding what was clean and unclean and how they used these human traditions to set aside the commandments of God. Then He spoke to the people about what truly made them unclean, and He didn't mince words:

This is all consistent with what Jesus said about the human heart.

> **For from within, out of the heart of man, come evil thoughts, sexual immorality, theft, murder, adultery, coveting, wickedness, deceit, sensuality, envy, slander, pride, foolishness. All these evil things come from within, and they defile a person. (MARK 7:21–23)**

Jesus certainly does not direct us to find true identity, meaning, and purpose within ourselves.

To drive this point home, I've sometimes asked a group of people to imagine that I have acquired some amazing new technology that allows me to gain access to all their thoughts from the last week and turn them into a short movie that I can now project in front of everyone. Usually, people chuckle, starting to get the point. Then I ask for a volunteer, and generally things go quiet as people consider for a split second what it would be like if the technology did exist. "All these evil things come from within, and they defile a person."

CURVED IN

It's not only that when we look in, we discover a mess of sin and evil; it is also the problem that we are obsessed with the very act of looking in. Martin Luther, following Augustine, spoke of the tendency of fallen humanity to be constantly turned in on ourselves—*incurvatus in se*, to use the Latin phrase. This is translated quite nicely as "curvedness" in the English edition of *Luther's Works*. Luther says:

> **[Scripture] describes man as so turned in on himself that he uses not only physical but even spiritual goods for his own purposes and in all things seeks only himself.**

> **This curvedness is now natural for us, a natural wickedness and a natural sinfulness.**[6]

Curvedness is a powerful picture of our sinful predicament and is helpful in thinking about the trend of expressive individualism.

Luther also links this to a Hebrew word from the Old Testament that is most commonly translated as "iniquity" but has the root sense of "crookedness." Sin distorts, bends, twists, and contorts. Luther also points to the woman in Luke 13:11, who was "bent over" and bound by Satan for eighteen years. Her devastating physical condition, Luther says, is a picture of our curved-in spiritual condition, and like the woman, we can be delivered only by the grace of God. To put it in the language of this book, our looking in is a far more serious problem than we might initially think. Lifting our eyes to look up and look out is not simply a change in habit or an act of the will; it happens only by the grace and power of God.

Lifting our eyes to look up and look out is not simply a change in habit or an act of the will; it happens only by the grace and power of God.

This means that between our sinful nature and the cultural trends, we're in something of a perfect storm. Our sinful nature leaves us curved in on ourselves, and the world around us now encourages us to answer life's big questions according to what we find inside. It bears repeating that this impacts everyone, including Christians. Even without realizing it, we slip into this mode, like the daughter in our opening scene.

6 *Luther's Works*, vol. 25, p. 345.

It's my experience that when people have some of this language and framework in mind, they begin to see these sorts of dynamics everywhere. I came across one profound example of this in pop culture in a song called "Look Inside Yourself" from the British band Hear'Say. Here is a quote from the chorus, which repeats throughout the song:

> The truth is only you can make you happy
> The thing is you know what you want
> Baby though, way deep down somewhere you've got all the answers
> There's something you need to know
> Look inside yourself.

These lyrics sum up the trends I've been discussing in this chapter and are about as diametrically opposed to the Christian worldview as one can get. The answers to life's big questions are not deep down somewhere inside yourself. The life of blessing is not found by turning inward. On the contrary, we find the answers and blessing we seek by lifting our eyes to our gracious God and looking out to those He has called us to serve.

REFLECTION QUESTIONS

1. Do you agree that people tend to look inward to find identity, purpose, and meaning?

2. Where and how have you seen expressive individualism at work both in the world around you and in the Christian community?

3. Read Jeremiah 17:9; Romans 7:21; and Mark 7:21–23. What do these verses teach us about our inner life? Do these verses resonate with your experience?

4. How do you still struggle with being curved in on yourself?

5. How might the father from the opening of the chapter begin to speak to his daughter about her struggles?

CHAPTER 2

LOOKING UP AND LOOKING OUT

The Dynamic

For this reason, because I have heard of your faith in the Lord Jesus and your love toward all the saints, I do not cease to give thanks for you, remembering you in my prayers.

Ephesians 1:15–16

UP AND OUT

For most of my childhood, I was very blessed to have four living grandparents who were examples to me in faith and life. They were Christian people who regularly attended worship, were very involved in the life of the church, engaged with their community, loved their families, and worked hard. My grandparents on both sides of the family were farmers, so I have many fond memories of visiting them on their farms during school holidays and absorbing their way of life, even as a city slicker myself.

As I think about how Luther's theology helps us envisage a life different from the one commonly promoted in the world around us, I think of my grandparents. Even though they were thoughtful people, I don't think they spent much time looking inward to answer questions about identity and purpose. They looked up to God for all they needed and looked out to what needed to be done and got on with it. I'm incredibly grateful that this orientation in life was further modeled and instilled in me by my own father and mother. Looking up in faith and thanksgiving. Looking out in love and service.

In this chapter, I lay out an alternative to looking in, a vision for the life God gives us as Christians in this world: looking up and looking out. We'll explore this especially using insights from Martin Luther and other reformers—although, as mentioned earlier, most Christians should find much to agree with here. Behind the idea of looking up and looking out is a dimension of Luther's theology called the two kinds of righteousness. This paradigm has received renewed attention in recent decades by contemporary Lutheran theologians, such as Robert Kolb, who have helpfully reflected on how the two kinds of righteousness can speak to concerns we face today. My work stands on the shoulders of these theologians.

Behind the idea of looking up and looking out is a dimension of Luther's theology called the two kinds of righteousness.

There are several features of the two kinds of righteousness paradigm. In this chapter, I'll cover four of these features, which will serve as the theological groundwork for the rest of the book. The first is that we live in two realms—before God and before the world. The second is that we are rightly related in these two realms in different ways—namely, by receiving Christ's own righteousness as a gift (one kind of righteousness) and by following His example in serving others (a second kind of righteousness). The third feature is that faith and love are the main characteristics of our relationships in this paradigm—faith in our relation to God and love in our relation to others. Finally, then, the fourth feature is that the vision of life offered in these two dimensions can help us understand what it is to be truly human, an important, constructive use of this theology for our confused times.

TWO REALMS

What is the reality in which we live as human beings? Some might say that all that exists is what we can see and touch. At the other extreme, people might think this whole world we perceive is an illusion of one sort or another. And when it comes to God, even those who do acknowledge His existence can imagine that in different ways. Perhaps God exists but is so far removed from this life that His existence is basically irrelevant day-to-day. Or people may imagine that God is actually more like the life force flowing through all things, and so, in the end, there's really no difference between relating to God and relating to this world.

In the Western world for the last few hundred years, disbelieving in God or in any transcendent reality has become increasingly common. People live without a sense that all of life is lived in the presence of God. Our conversation partner from the last chapter, Charles Taylor, has another helpful expression that gets at this phenomenon. He speaks of modern people living in an "immanent frame." This describes the conceptual or metaphorical moral space of a secular age, the unseen cultural mindset that frames our thinking and lives. The immanent frame tends to close people off from the transcendent because all purpose, meaning, and significance—or what Taylor likes to call "fullness"—can theoretically be found within this frame rather than outside it.

In contrast, Lutheran theologians often speak of human life in this world as existing in two realms: in the presence of God and in the presence of other people.[7] This distinction is the first feature of the two kinds of righteousness paradigm. That we live in the presence of other people is an empirical fact and obvious to all. Although even here, there are ways in which we can fail to appreciate how truly interdependent we are in this life and how much we need relationships and human community. More on this later. Nevertheless, the fact that we live before other people in this life is the less controversial reality of these two realms. It is the other realm—life before God—that is less obvious to people nowadays. Yet, this is a fundamental aspect of the Christian faith.

Being in the presence of God first became a problem after the fall into sin (Genesis 3:8), when Adam and Eve hid themselves from His presence in shame. They were then driven out of the

7 I am using the language of two realms following the usage of Robert Kolb, who deals with the same reality often spoken of as Luther's two kingdoms but from the perspective of the human person. Thus, whereas authors have traditionally spoken of the two kingdoms in terms of God's two ways of ruling His world, Kolb often speaks of human life taking place in a realm of relationship with God and in a quite distinct realm of relationships with God's creatures. See Robert Kolb, "Luther's Hermeneutics of Distinctions: Law and Gospel, Two Kinds of Righteousness, Two Realms, Freedom and Bondage," in *The Oxford Handbook of Martin Luther's Theology*, ed. Robert Kolb, Irene Dingel, and L'ubomír Batka (Oxford University Press, 2014), 164–84.

garden and could no longer enjoy Eden's perfect communion with God and each other. Yet, this does not mean God abandoned His creation. The Scriptures consistently reveal that human beings continue to live under the watchful eye of their Creator. For example, we read:

> **Where shall I go from Your Spirit? Or where shall I flee from Your presence? If I ascend to heaven, You are there! If I make my bed in Sheol, You are there! (Psalm 139:7–8)**

In the Bible, the problem is not whether we are aware of being in God's presence—that is taken for granted—but whether that is good news or bad. This is also where the concept of the two kinds of righteousness is very helpful, as we'll come to shortly.

Thinking in terms of these two realms makes clear that we are always both in the presence of God and in the presence of other human beings. Here, we might also think of our Lord Jesus, who summarized life lived according to God's Law as loving God and loving neighbor (Matthew 22:37–40), pointing to this twofold dynamic as He conversed with the Pharisees. We can note as well how Paul uses language evocative of these two realms in his charge to Timothy. He first notes how Timothy made his good confession "in the presence of many witnesses"—human witnesses, that is—and then charges him to faithfulness "in the presence of God" (1 Timothy 6:12–14).

We are always both in the presence of God and in the presence of other human beings.

In theological circles, this reality is sometimes discussed using Latin phrases. The average reader may wonder why academics feel the need to do this. As a student, I heard jokes about professors using German or Latin to deflect difficult questions! However, using Latin here draws attention to the fact that these are technical terms, specific phrases the reformers intentionally used in the original writings. The Latin phrases are *coram Deo*, "before or in the presence of God," and *coram mundo*, "before or in the presence of the world." An alternative for *coram mundo* is *coram hominibus*, meaning "before people." Once you realize that this is axiomatic in Lutheran thinking, you begin to notice it everywhere, and many things fall into place.

Let me offer an example from my own experience. My piety has been shaped significantly by the liturgical heritage of the Lutheran Church of Australia. The rite of confession and absolution in the Divine Service in that tradition asks three questions:

> **I ask each of you in the presence of God who searches the heart: Do you confess that you have sinned, and do you repent of your sins?**
>
> **Do you believe that Jesus Christ has redeemed you from all your sins, and do you desire forgiveness in his name?**
>
> **Do you intend with the help of the Holy Spirit to live as in God's presence, and to strive to lead a holy life, even as Christ has made you holy?**[8]

To my knowledge, these questions have not been a prominent part of North American Lutheranism, but they come to mind for me as I think about life in two realms. The questions emphasize that all of life is lived in God's presence. After being absolved, we are encouraged to set out into our daily lives once again to

8 *Lutheran Hymnal with Supplement* (Openbook Publishers, 1989), 6.

love and serve our neighbor while still always acknowledging that this is done *coram Deo.*

A common way of communicating this reality of the two realms is to speak of the vertical and horizontal dimensions of life. A helpful visual is to picture a person with one line going up to symbolize *coram Deo* and another going out to the side for *coram hominibus.* We imagine God above us and fellow human beings beside us. The life of a human person exists simultaneously before God and before others. The idea of lifting our eyes draws on this visual and spatial way of thinking—looking up to God and looking out to our neighbor.

It's important to say at this point that we can't divide our lives neatly into these two realms as if they don't overlap and interrelate. It's not as if on Sunday morning at worship we are in the presence of God and not in the presence of others and that we are before the world the rest of the week and not before God. Our earthly life as husband, wife, brother, sister, or friend does not suddenly cease when we are at prayer. And even more important, as we serve our neighbor, we do so always in the presence of God. These two realms are a simultaneous part of our reality as human beings. There's a dynamic relationship between them rather than something static and separated.

Lifting our eyes draws on this visual and spatial way of thinking.

TWO KINDS OF RIGHTEOUSNESS

With the two realms in mind, we can now discuss the second distinction and feature of this paradigm: the two kinds of righteousness, or how we stand in a right relation to God and to other people. Luther and the other reformers point out that the way we are righteous *coram Deo* is different from the way we are righteous *coram hominibus*. The Christian is righteous before God purely by God's gracious action in Christ and receives this as a gift. The Christian then is active in his or her righteousness with other people through love and service.

Let's trace this theme through Luther and other Lutheran confessional writings. In the Book of Concord, original sin is defined as the loss of original righteousness, and original righteousness is defined as the ability to love God above all things and keep His Commandments.[9] The Apology of the Augsburg Confession, one of the Reformation's earliest confessional documents, includes this understanding of what righteousness means in the Bible:

> **In the Scriptures, righteousness consists not only in obeying the Second Table of the Ten Commandments ‹which are about good works in serving our fellowman›, but also the First Table, which teaches about fearing God, faith, and loving God. Therefore, original righteousness includes not only physical health in all ways . . . but also these gifts: a sure and certain knowledge of God, fear of God, confidence in God, and the desire and ability to give God these things. Scripture testifies to this when it says in Genesis 1:27 that man was made in the image and likeness of God. What else was this image and likeness other than that man was created with wisdom and righteousness so that he could apprehend God and reflect God?**[10]

9 Apology of the Augsburg Confession, Article 2, paragraphs 15–16.

10 Apology of the Augsburg Confession, Article 2, paragraphs 16–18. Brackets in original.

There are two features to note here. First is the theme of duality running through the text as it speaks of loving God *and* keeping His Commandments, of the *two* tables of the Decalogue, and of original righteousness as both grasping *and* reflecting God. Second is that the truth of God's good creation sits behind the discussion of original righteousness and original sin, and so original righteousness could be described as human life in God's design.

Luther speaks about the two kinds of righteousness in various places, but most famously in a sermon by that title and later in his Galatians commentary. In his sermon, he calls the pair "alien righteousness," which is righteousness that comes from another, and "proper righteousness," which is righteousness that is one's own. Alien righteousness is Christ's righteousness, given to Christians as a gift and received by faith and in Baptism. Proper righteousness is the life of love and good works. Luther argues that this distinction gives the motivation for Christians to love their neighbor, as they have the righteousness of Christ and no longer need to seek that righteousness before God on their own.

This distinction gives the motivation for Christians to love their neighbor.

Much later in his career, Luther is still using the language of two kinds of righteousness in his Galatians commentary. Luther writes, "We set forth two worlds, as it were, one of them heavenly and the other earthly. Into these we place these two kinds of righteousness, which are distinct and separated from each other."[11] Here, Luther speaks first of two worlds (which is another way of expressing the two-realms distinction) and

11 *Luther's Works*, vol. 26, p. 8.

then says there are two different kinds of righteousness located in these two worlds. While the two realms overlap and interact dynamically, the two kinds of righteousness operate distinctly. He also speaks very strongly about the significance of the two kinds of righteousness for his whole outlook:

> **This is our theology, by which we teach a precise distinction between these two kinds of righteousness, the active and the passive, so that morality and faith, works and grace, secular society and religion may not be confused. Both are necessary, but both must be kept within their limits.**[12]

Luther uses the language of passive and active righteousness to emphasize that, fundamentally, the Christian is passive before God in receiving Christ's righteousness as a gift and active toward the neighbor in living out the righteousness of love.

I mentioned that the two kinds of righteousness appear in the early documents of the Book of Concord. The terminology also appears in the Formula of Concord, which was written much later. There, in the article about how Christ's divine and human natures relate to His gift of righteousness to us, the reformers write:

> **It is also correct to say that believers who have been justified through faith in Christ first have the righteousness of faith credited to them in this life. Then, they also have the initial righteousness of the new obedience or of good works. But these two types of righteousness must not be mixed with each other or both be injected into**

12 *Luther's Works*, vol. 26, p. 7.

> **the article of justification by faith before God. For this initial righteousness or renewal in us is incomplete and impure in this life because of the flesh. A person cannot stand with and ‹on the ground of this righteousness› before God's court.**[13]

Here, we see how Lutherans continued using this paradigm after Luther himself, both in their terminology and in their caution against confusing and mixing these two kinds of righteousness.

FAITH AND LOVE

We see, then, that we live in two realms as human beings in this world, and when we are rightly related to God and neighbor, we live in a twofold state of righteousness. This also means that our life before God and our life before others are characterized in two different ways. We inhabit these two realms differently. Here, I refer to the pair of faith and love, the third feature of this paradigm. Before God, we live primarily by faith, which passively receives the alien righteousness of Christ. Before other people, we live primarily by love, which actively serves and so develops a proper righteousness. In other words, this pair of faith and love correlates to the *coram Deo* and *coram mundo* pair and the two kinds of righteousness. I will talk in later chapters about how faith and love don't exhaust our relations in those spheres—in fact, there is an important place for active praise and thanksgiving toward God. However, faith and love are fundamental in these two realms and sets of relationships.

13 Solid Declaration of the Formula of Concord, Article 3, paragraph 32. Brackets in original.

They are like the fulcrum on which other facets of our Christian life turn.

This emphasis on faith and love comes out strongly in various writings from Luther and in the Lutheran Confessions. Let's look first at Luther's tract "The Freedom of a Christian." Toward the end, he asserts:

> **We conclude, therefore, that a Christian lives not in himself, but in Christ and in his neighbor. Otherwise he is not a Christian. He lives in Christ through faith, in his neighbor through love. By faith he is caught up beyond himself into God. By love he descends beneath himself into his neighbor.**[14]

That quote is another thread of inspiration for this book. For Luther, faith and love are more than just two facets of life; the Christian life consists of these in a fundamental way. He contrasts this with a life lived *in oneself*, which is the problem we discussed in chapter 1 with expressive individualism and our sinful nature. The Christian life is one in which we're called outside of ourselves both as we look up to God in faith and as we look out to our neighbor in love.

We're called outside of ourselves both as we look up to God in faith and as we look out to our neighbor in love.

The passage from Ephesians that opened this chapter features this same pair. Paul thanks his heavenly Father for the people's *faith* in the Lord Jesus and their *love* for all the saints. He says the same when he writes to the Colossians (Colossians 1:4). And Paul reminds the Galatians that "in Christ Jesus neither

14 *Luther's Works*, vol. 31, p. 371.

circumcision nor uncircumcision counts for anything, but only faith working through love" (Galatians 5:6). The apostle John writes similarly, handing on God's instruction: "And this is His commandment, that we believe in the name of His Son Jesus Christ and love one another, just as He has commanded us" (1 John 3:23). Over and over again we find these pairs: God and neighbor, faith and love.

In my own experience as a Christian, the pair of faith and love takes my mind to one of the post-Communion prayers in the liturgy, when the congregation thanks God for the body and blood of Christ in the Sacrament. There, we ask that it would strengthen us "in faith toward You and in fervent love toward one another."[15] I've always found this a helpful focus as we move toward the end of the Divine Service and prepare to be sent out with God's blessing. The Scripture readings, sermon, hymns, and prayers may have brought many different themes, truths, and possibilities to mind. But in this prayer for God's strength in faith toward Him and love toward others, we have a prism through which to view the meditations of the last hour or so and return to our daily callings.

Over and over again we find these pairs: God and neighbor, faith and love.

TRULY AND FULLY HUMAN

This brings us to the fourth feature of Luther's two kinds of righteousness paradigm. Earlier, I mentioned that contemporary Lutheran theologians have revived much interest in this concept.

---

15 *Lutheran Service Book*, p. 166.

The main person leading the way has been Robert Kolb of Concordia Seminary, St. Louis. One of Kolb's major contributions as he reflects on this theology for today is to suggest that the concept of two kinds of righteousness is Luther's understanding of what it is to be truly or fully human. For Luther, faith and love encompass what it means to have true life as a Christian person. Kolb calls this the "two-dimensional definition of humanity at the heart of [Luther's] theology." Kolb writes:

> **Martin Luther knew *how* he was righteous *where*; he knew *where* he was truly human *in what manner*. That is, he recognized that being human in God's sight means receiving the unconditional love of God. It means child-like dependence, expressed in the absolute trust of complete love. Furthermore, Luther recognized that being human in relationship to the creatures of God meant the exercise of adult responsibility as God designed it for human creatures, expressed in the care and concern of deeds of complete love for others.**[16]

Kolb draws on many aspects of Luther's thought to arrive at this conclusion but especially on Luther's Genesis lectures, in which he investigates God's original creation of human beings and what that means. An important aspect of this has to do with how vital relationships are to human beings.

A family I knew had a son who was having a lot of challenges settling into his new school. The formerly happy kid was now often sad, grumpy, angry, and unmotivated when it came to

16 Robert Kolb, "Luther on the Two Kinds of Righteousness; Reflections on His Two-Dimensional Definition of Humanity at the Heart of His Theology," *Lutheran Quarterly*, no. 13 (1999): 455. Emphasis original.

attending school. His parents and teachers were very much invested in helping him and so looked at different options. The boy underwent some psychological testing, and they discussed the possibility of different medications. However, shortly after that, things changed for the better. His general outlook improved at home and at school, and so did his grades. His parents and teachers gradually realized that what had changed was very simple—he had made some friends. In the end, one of his deepest needs was not appropriate therapy for psychological trauma or medical intervention for chemical imbalance but quality relationships. This is so often the way it is for human beings. We need relationships. That's why being truly human must, at its core, mean being rightly related first to God and then to other people.

The concept of two kinds of righteousness is Luther's understanding of what it is to be truly or fully human.

This expansion of Luther's two kinds of righteousness helps us utilize Reformation insights to address the cultural problems we experience today. Expressive individualism is not only about the expression of personal preferences in itself but also about doing it as a way of realizing one's very humanity. Kolb's work, building on Luther, offers us an alternative, Christian vision for what true humanity is according to God's design. The outlook of expressive individualism desires to answer the big questions of life by turning inward, but for Christians, turning outward to God and neighbor is a better way to go.

The rest of this book offers my take on this vision. The spiritual posture of looking up and looking out helps us orient ourselves as Christians surrounded by expressive individualism.

As we lift our eyes to look up to God and out to our neighbor, we find true life and answers to the big questions of who we are and why we are here.

Reflection Questions

1. How difficult do you think it is for people in the modern world to acknowledge they live in the presence of God?

2. How difficult do you think it is for Christians today to live "as in the presence of God"?

3. In what ways do people confuse the two kinds of righteousness?

4. How important do you think relationships are to being human?

5. What does the dynamic of faith and love look like in your daily life?

PART 2

Christian Living as Lifting Our Eyes

CHAPTER 3

LOOKING UP IN FAITH

The Heart and Center

For this is the will of My Father, that everyone who looks on the Son and believes in Him should have eternal life, and I will raise him up on the last day.

John 6:40

WHO AM I? AM I WORTHY?

A man talked to a friend about his life and how he had strayed from his Christian upbringing. He hadn't been to church in many years. He had really made a mess of things in his family and was not proud of what he had done. Recently, though, things had happened that prompted him to reexamine his life and consider the Christian faith of his youth. He had started trying to pray and read the Bible at home, although with some trepidation.

The friend listened, talked, and encouraged the man in all this. He reminded his friend that all Christians are sinners who need God's forgiveness and that no one is beyond God's grace. At a certain point, he shared about his congregation and invited the man to come along to a service.

The man responded, "I don't mean to be dramatic, but if I go in there, the roof might just fall in! I don't know how God could ever accept someone like me."

Another man came to speak to a pastor, as he was also interested in coming back to church after a long time away. Even though he hadn't been connected to a church for a long time, he saw himself as a Christian person. Eventually, the man shared with the pastor that he identified as a gay man and was unsure what this meant for his life as a Christian. The pastor held to the scriptural teaching about the sinfulness of homosexual activity but decided not to jump there too quickly. Instead, he continued to listen to the man and learn more about his life.

As the man spoke, it became clear that he was not sexually active and was not particularly interested in becoming so. He had simply found friendship with and a certain degree of acceptance by men in that community. As such, he identified as a gay man. As they talked, the pastor discerned that the man's self-identification was the place to begin his spiritual diagnosis and engagement. He gently challenged the man about what it was that truly defined him. The man claimed to be a Christian. Surely, the core identity of anyone professing to be a Christian is child of God, even as they struggle with different temptations, sexual and otherwise.

Questions of identity and who we are as human beings dominate discussion in our culture today. We are often encouraged, implicitly or explicitly, to look inward to answer these questions. This has become so common that people can now easily complete the sentence "I am . . ." by listing their career, a character trait, their race or nationality, or even something to do with their sexuality. Consider the simple yet profound difference between saying "I work as a lawyer" and "I *am* a lawyer." We speak of certain aspects of life as if they are the core of our identity. But as Christians, we are called to look first and foremost to what God says and does as constituting reality for us, including for our identity.

As Christians, we are called to look first and foremost to what God says and does as constituting reality for us.

In addition to this desire to define who we are by ourselves rather than receiving our identity from God, there is also the deeper spiritual problem of our guilt and shame before God. This shame can cause us to flee from God's presence like Adam and Eve or the man in the first story I shared. Our guilt and shame before God are real. From the point of view of our own sinfulness, each of us is indeed unworthy to stand before a holy God. Yet this is why Christianity is such good news! In Jesus, God forgives our sin, covers our shame, and restores us to a right relationship with Himself through faith. We are given a new identity and a new standing before God. This is the passive righteousness we began to explore in the last chapter. It is the heart and center of the Christian life as we *look up* to God in faith and so receive a new status and identity as forgiven and loved children of God.

LOOKING TO THE WORK OF CHRIST

God's people have always lived before Him based on His mercy and forgiveness rather than their own worthiness. Several times, the people of Israel are told something like the following:

> **It was not because you were more in number than any other people that the LORD set His love on you and chose you, for you were the fewest of all peoples, but it**

> **is because the LORD loves you and is keeping the oath that He swore to your fathers, that the LORD has brought you out with a mighty hand and redeemed you from the house of slavery, from the hand of Pharaoh king of Egypt. (DEUTERONOMY 7:7–8)**

From beginning to end, the Scriptures tell the story of how God takes the initiative in loving, choosing, and saving His people.

In a rather mysterious scene of the Old Testament, God sent poisonous snakes among the people as punishment for their grumbling against Him. The people repented, and then we read, "So Moses made a bronze serpent and set it on a pole. And if a serpent bit anyone, he would *look* at the bronze serpent and live" (Numbers 21:9, emphasis added). The people themselves were not able to do anything to reverse the effects of their sin. Instead, in His mercy, the Lord provided what was needed for their healing and deliverance from death. The people were asked to look up in faith to what God had provided as the means for their salvation.

Jesus draws an explicit connection between this event and His own coming and work in the world. He says, "And as Moses lifted up the serpent in the wilderness, so must the Son of Man be lifted up, that whoever believes in Him may have eternal life" (John 3:14–15). In the Old Testament event, God provided a serpent set on a pole to which the people looked and were saved. Jesus says this pointed forward to God sending Him as the means by which people can be saved from all sin and eternal death. However, the connection is not only in the mere provision of a means for salvation but especially in what happens with the serpent or the Son being "lifted up." It is not only that Christ comes but, more important, what He comes to do. Later in John's Gospel, it is made clear that this lifting up refers especially to Jesus' death on the cross (John 12:32–33). There is also a secondary sense in which He is lifted up in His resurrection from the dead and ascension to the Father's right hand.

Notice, too, that whereas the people of old were to look at the serpent, Jesus says people are to believe in the Son of Man. Jesus interprets the looking of the people of old as an expression of faith in what God had provided and promised. Jesus also brings together the language of looking and believing in relation to Himself in another passage of John's Gospel, saying, "For this is the will of My Father, that everyone who looks on the Son and believes in Him should have eternal life, and I will raise him up on the last day" (John 6:40). For us, this is a call to look with the eyes of faith to Jesus and His work for us. But the people to whom Jesus spoke would literally look at Him being lifted up on the cross. As John will point out during Christ's Passion, "these things took place that the Scripture might be fulfilled: . . . 'They will look on Him whom they have pierced'" (John 19:36, 37).

For us, this is a call to look with the eyes of faith to Jesus and His work for us.

TRUE WORTHINESS

The work of Christ—chiefly His death and resurrection—brings redemption to the world. But how does a person individually receive the benefits of this? The man we met at the beginning of this chapter, for example, who wouldn't even step into a church for fear of the roof collapsing, was not concerned with the world's worthiness; he questioned whether he himself was worthy. The Scriptures teach that a person receives the benefits of Christ's work of redemption by believing in Him—looking to Him—and is thus restored to a right relationship with God. This is the righteousness of faith that we looked at earlier, the passive, alien kind of righteousness.

This righteousness of faith is closely linked to the central teaching of the Lutheran Reformation: justification by faith alone. The Augsburg Confession articulates it like this:

> **Our churches teach that people cannot be justified before God by their own strength, merits, or works. People are freely justified for Christ's sake, through faith, when they believe that they are received into favor and that their sins are forgiven for Christ's sake. By His death, Christ made satisfaction for our sins. God counts this faith for righteousness in His sight (Romans 3 and 4).**[17]

That articulation is based on Romans 3–4. It's worth reading this key passage in full:

> **But now the righteousness of God has been manifested apart from the law, although the Law and the Prophets bear witness to it—the righteousness of God through faith in Jesus Christ for all who believe. For there is no distinction: for all have sinned and fall short of the glory of God, and are justified by His grace as a gift, through the redemption that is in Christ Jesus, whom God put forward as a propitiation by His blood, to be received by faith. This was to show God's righteousness, because in His divine forbearance He had passed over former sins.**

17 Article 4.

> **It was to show His righteousness at the present time, so that He might be just and the justifier of the one who has faith in Jesus. (ROMANS 3:21–26)**

In the original Greek of the New Testament, the terms translated as "justification" and "righteousness" are very close. They are variations of the same word, so that to be justified is to be righteous-fied, in improper English. So, as Luther spoke of the two kinds of righteousness, and especially the passive kind of righteousness that avails before God, he was speaking about the reality of justification in slightly different terms.

To be justified is to be put right with God, to be declared just and innocent before Him. To put it in words closer to the situation of the man discussed earlier, to be justified is to become worthy of being in God's presence. The Scriptures and the teaching of the Augsburg Confession make clear that this does not happen because of anything we do; it is only ever a gift of God's grace, which is received in faith. The man fearful of the roof falling in needs to hear that because Jesus shed His blood for him on the cross, he can be put right with God by believing in Him. And even this faith is not something the man must do; it is more like the empty hands that receive a gift. In his final words before he died, Luther famously described us as spiritual beggars. We all come before God with nothing in our hands to offer Him that can atone for our sin, but because Christ has done that for us, we can passively receive the gift of His righteousness and so stand before Him confidently and joyfully.

To be justified is to become worthy of being in God's presence.

WORD AND SACRAMENTS

One possible misunderstanding of the spiritual posture of looking up is to imagine God is only somewhere up in a distant heaven, as if our faith is a spiritual long-distance relationship. This is not the way it is with God's presence or what it means to have faith though. The incarnation of Jesus means definitively that God is near to us in this world. Jesus says He will be with us always (Matthew 28:20). In Lutheran theology, we are especially pointed to God's Word and Sacraments as the means by which God is present with us in this life. Justification, or being made right with God, is not a one-off event that has no further bearing on the Christian life. Like any relationship, it is an ongoing reality. We lift our eyes to God in faith, especially as we return to the promises of our Baptism and gather in God's presence for Divine Service.

In Baptism, we are united to Christ's death and resurrection and so receive the benefits of His saving work. Our heavenly Father adopts us as His beloved children and gives us the gift of the Holy Spirit. This is one dimension of our Christian life that especially speaks to modern confusion about questions of identity. Paul addresses this quite directly in the book of Galatians, saying, "For as many of you as were baptized into Christ have put on Christ. There is neither Jew nor Greek, there is neither slave nor free, there is no male and female, for you are all one in Christ Jesus" (Galatians 3:27–28). In the context of questions of race and nationality, gender and sexuality, or work and career status in the world—all ways we still seek to define ourselves today—Paul points Christians to their Baptism into Christ as what defines them. The man from earlier in the chapter who struggled with his sexuality is first and foremost a baptized child of the heavenly Father. When we start with that core identity, other issues come into different perspective.

As we gather in God's presence for Divine Service, we gather as baptized people. We begin in the triune name into which we were baptized, trusting the promises of our heavenly Father, first received in our Baptism. We hear the word of forgiveness pronounced in the absolution, which is some of the clearest language declaring us put right with God. As we listen to God's Word in the Scriptures and the sermon, we are convicted of our failure to live according to God's Law, yet we also hear again the promises of the Gospel. As we celebrate the Lord's Supper, we hear our Lord's words of promise: "Take and eat, this is My body, given for you. This is My blood, shed for you for the forgiveness of sins." As the service concludes, we hear one of the rich blessings drawn from Scripture, perhaps of the Lord's looking on us with favor. The Divine Service calls us as Christian people to look up to God in faith to receive once again the blessings of His promises of forgiveness, life, and salvation.

The Divine Service calls us as Christian people to look up to God in faith to receive once again the blessings of His promises of forgiveness, life, and salvation.

All this isn't to say that it's only within the context of the Divine Service that we exercise our faith and look up to God to be renewed in who we are. The Christian is called daily to live in God's Word and often does so through personal Scripture reading or by gathering in small groups for Bible study, prayer, and mutual encouragement. As we read the Bible alone or with others, it can be the default to look for something we need to do based on a certain passage. There is nothing wrong with this;

God's Word certainly provides direction for our lives, and His Law is His expression of how we are to live. Yet, in addition to reading the Bible for moral instruction and guidance, it's even more important for us to be alert to the promises we read and hear in God's Word. Every promise is a call for our trust, and it is by this ongoing life of faith—looking up to Him—that we have true life in Christ.

RAISED HEADS AND HEARTS

So far, we have discussed looking up to God mainly in a metaphorical sense of looking up to God in faith. We also noted how John's Gospel illustrates a literal sense of looking up for those who looked upon Christ on the cross. As we consider the ongoing life of faith as we live in our Baptism, hear God's Word of forgiveness, and receive Christ's body and blood, there is also a literal sense of looking for us. Let me explain.

In the years I have been involved in the pastoral ministry, I have had the privilege to perform many Baptisms, preach many sermons, and conduct many Divine Services. It is a privilege because through these means God is at work delivering His gifts of forgiveness, life, and salvation to His people. As I have carried out my ministry through these activities, I can recall the many times people look up, both literally and in faith, to receive from God.

The infant is brought to the font by his or her Christian parents. The baby squirms and cries, looking around at the gathered congregation and the strange setting. But as the little one is baptized, they often look up at me as they hear the words and as the water drips down their head. Then sometimes they cry louder! As the Spirit works through the Word of promise in that child's Baptism, the very faith that receives God's work of salvation is being created. Even that simple looking up of the helpless infant is an image of the receptivity of faith through which God works.

As people confess their sins in worship, they often bow their heads in self-examination and as a gesture of repentance. "We confess that we have sinned . . ." However, as the time comes to pronounce the words of forgiveness from Christ Himself, I have noticed people often look up at that moment to receive this wonderful gift. As they look up at their pastor, they look with the eyes of faith to the One in whose stead the pastor stands—Christ Himself—and the gift of forgiveness declared.

As they look up at their pastor, they look with the eyes of faith to the One in whose stead the pastor stands–Christ Himself.

When listening to a sermon, people have different ways of hearing and meditating on God's Word. Some have their eyes fixed forward on the preacher almost the whole time. Others gaze slightly into the distance as they ponder the truths being proclaimed. Quite a few actually close their eyes for periods or look down. Yet when there are more pointed and direct proclamations of the Gospel and how it is *for you*, again, I'm struck that many faces look up to the pulpit. They look up to where that Gospel is being proclaimed to them, and as they do, they look up in faith to the God who declares them right and just in His sight through that very proclamation.

Something similar happens at Holy Communion. In most places I have served, the people come forward to kneel at the altar rail with heads slightly bowed in reverence for the precious gift of the body and blood of Jesus they are about to receive.

However, to actually receive this gift, one must raise one's head and look up slightly. As the words are spoken, "Take and eat, this is the body of Christ. Take and drink, this is the blood of Christ," people look up at the pastor distributing, even as they look up in faith to the very One they encounter in this Sacrament for their salvation.

There are other ways we literally look up and around in church too. Luther and many others in history realized that images and artwork can be especially helpful for children or others who, as modern people would put it, are more visual learners. In the congregations where I've served, the church buildings have all had stained glass windows depicting biblical scenes and other Christian artwork on display. I've often found myself pointing people, and especially children, to these images to reinforce a point of Christian teaching or supplement a lesson from Scripture. For example, one congregation had a central window depicting the ascension of our Lord into glory. As a person looked closely at the details, the nail marks in Christ's hands and feet were visible even as He shone with heavenly light. This became a visual prompt for the wonderful truth we learn in the Gospels, which is expressed memorably by the hymn writer: "Rich wounds, yet visible above, in beauty glorified."[18]

Sometimes, even in less inspiring spaces, visual aids can be brought in. In confirmation class, after explicit instruction on a Bible passage or a section of the catechism, I'll sometimes bring out one of my icons of Christ or another piece of artwork to discuss. I've often found it supplements the other teaching very well as young people look on an image and look with faith

18 Matthew Bridges, "Crown Him with Many Crowns," *Lutheran Service Book* 525:3.

to the One the image depicts. I'm convinced that God can use our literal eyes in connection with Christian artwork to grow us in faith through the eyes of our hearts.

As the people of God look up in faith to His giving of His gifts in the Divine Service, I sometimes think of our Lord's words from the Gospel of Luke, when He discusses His return in glory: "Now when these things begin to take place, straighten up and raise your heads, because your redemption is drawing near" (Luke 21:28). Our Lord encourages a spiritual posture of raised heads in anticipation of the consummation of all He has accomplished, and in the Divine Service, we cultivate this posture as we raise our heads and look in faith to where God gives His gifts.

We cultivate this posture as we raise our heads and look in faith to where God gives His gifts.

LOOKING TO JESUS

Each morning as I wake up, I haul my legs to the side of the bed and rub my eyes to slowly rouse myself. I'm often still tired from too little sleep. Perhaps I've been up tending a distressed child or a barking dog. If it's a particularly stressful period of life, sometimes even in those first moments, the pressures of the day will immediately begin to flood my mind and heart. So before I've really even gotten moving, my face may drop a little. However, I also try to remember Luther's counsel for morning prayer: As you get up, make the sign of the cross and say, "In the name of the Father and of the Son and of the Holy Spirit," then pray the Lord's Prayer and Luther's Morning Prayer. As I do this, I confess the triune God into whose name I was baptized and in whom I believe, and so entrust my day ahead to Him.

In doing so, I also confess who I am as His dearly loved child. As I do this, I begin to lift my eyes. I look up to God in trust that I have another day in front of me in which, no matter what happens, He has reconciled me to Himself and dwells with me.

Modern people are preoccupied with figuring out their identity, struggling to understand who they are and what they are worth. Yet paradoxically, we find secure answers to our questions of identity or worthiness not by looking in at ourselves but rather by looking up to Christ and what He has done for us. The writer to the Hebrews provides perhaps the best expression of this spiritual posture as a defining dimension of the Christian life. Lift your eyes to Christ and be encouraged by these words:

> **Therefore, since we are surrounded by so great a cloud of witnesses, let us also lay aside every weight, and sin which clings so closely, and let us run with endurance the race that is set before us, *looking* to Jesus, the founder and perfecter of our faith, who for the joy that was set before Him endured the cross, despising the shame, and is seated at the right hand of the throne of God. (Hebrews 12:1–2, emphasis added)**

Reflection Questions

1. Have you met anyone like the two people in the opening anecdotes? Share those experiences and how you handled them.

2. Where do you think many people look to find a sense of identity today?

3. Why is it so important to keep clear and central that our righteousness before God is always passively received rather than earned?

4. When during worship do you tend to lower or lift your eyes? How might this be significant?

5. How does the artwork or design in your church help or hinder your ability to look up to where Christ's promises are being delivered to you?

CHAPTER 4

LOOKING UP IN THANKSGIVING

The Joyful Response

Then He ordered the crowds to sit down on the grass, and taking the five loaves and the two fish, He looked up to heaven and said a blessing. Then He broke the loaves and gave them to the disciples, and the disciples gave them to the crowds.

MATTHEW 14:19

THE VALUE OF GRATITUDE

Why are we so insistent on teaching our children to say thank you? In my experience, you will find this habit the world over. Parents will follow the offer of food, drink, or a toy with the prompt, "Say thank you now . . ." We learn these basic manners by echoing our parents. As children get slightly older, parents will often intervene if a child forgets to say thank you to others. The shop assistant might even participate in the ritual, withholding the item briefly until the child follows the parent's instruction to say thank you. Even if we can't articulate exactly why saying thank you is so important, most parents intuitively know there is something profound involved that can't be neglected.

We end up teaching this over and over to children because they simply won't do it naturally, even if they've come to understand the concept. When discussing this theme, I sometimes ask parents when they have needed to teach their children to be demanding and have a sense of entitlement. Some look at me confused; those who catch on quicker smile or laugh. Of course, no one ever needs to teach a child to be demanding—that comes naturally. We do need to teach them to be thankful and to express it. In the early years, we settle for developing the habit and hope the true sentiment behind it will take root later on.

We also feel the need to emphasize saying thank you for another reason. This comes into focus when we consider that we don't teach our children to say thank you to vending machines.[19] We don't give our children a few dollars, help them push the correct combination of letters and numbers for a candy bar, and then prompt them to say thank you to the vending machine. Why is that? It's not just the financial transaction; we still teach our children to say thank you to those serving us in a restaurant, after all. That contrast between a person and a machine shows us that saying thank you is also about relationships. As we thank someone, we acknowledge who they are and express our respect for them. Our relationship to God has a similar dynamic. As we look up in thanksgiving to Him, we acknowledge who He is and what He's given us and so grow in our relationship with Him.

As we thank someone, we acknowledge who they are and express our respect for them.

19 I'm indebted to Rev. Fraser Pearce for this illustration.

THANKSGIVING IN THE MODERN WORLD

The response of thanksgiving to God for what He has done for us is one that even Christians can sometimes skip over in their lives of faith. One reason for this is that we can over-emphasize the sort of paradigm I laid out earlier of faith and love. I find thinking of the Christian life around the fulcrum of faith toward God and love toward others very helpful. Yet it is not the whole story. There is a danger of reductionism here. When that happens, we can begin to think our only response to God's justifying and forgiving work in our lives is to love our neighbors. As important as that is, it risks missing this other crucial dimension of how we look up to God. We look up in faith to receive His gifts, but then we also joyfully look up in thanksgiving for those gifts.

Another reason we may underemphasize thanksgiving to God is because of the cultural pressure that Charles Taylor noted, our closed-off sense of existence in the immanent frame. While we might hold on to a sense of being in the presence of God in terms of how we stand as guilty or innocent, the overwhelming culture of immanence can crowd in again when it comes to our response to God's action for us. Interestingly, people still live with a sense of gratitude in the immanent frame, even if they profess not to believe in God—consider phenomena like the gratitude journal, which encourages people to write down what they are thankful for each day. While there is something good about this and it offers a potential contact point for Christian faith, the big question for Christians is not whether we *feel* thankful but rather *to whom* we give thanks.

ALL OF LIFE IS A GIFT

Throughout the Bible, God's people are encouraged and instructed to give thanks to Him. The reason behind that thankfulness often goes unstated; it is so fundamental to the biblical worldview that it can simply be assumed. The calls to thanksgiving in the Bible presuppose that all of life is a gift from God. This is contrary to what we might call the Bart Simpson view of the world. In an episode of *The Simpsons*, when asked to say grace, Bart obnoxiously says, "Dear God, we paid for all this stuff ourselves, so thanks for nothing."[20] One of the reasons *The Simpsons* was so popular was the way it succinctly and comically voiced some of the most prevalent and easily recognizable attitudes and trends of the day. The food on our table does not simply fall from heaven but rather comes to us through a complex network of human activity. As such, we can easily forget its ultimate source.

There are occasions in the Bible, though, where this presupposition of life is made more explicit. The apostle James says, "Every good gift and every perfect gift is from above, coming down from the Father of lights, with whom there is no variation or shadow due to change" (James 1:17). James knows that people buy items with money they've earned, that parents pass things down to children, that friends give gifts to one another. He knows that there are innumerable human

James confesses the truth that behind all this is the Father, who is the great gift-giver.

---

20 *The Simpsons*, season 2, episode 4, "Two Cars in Every Garage and Three Eyes on Every Fish," written by Sam Simon and John Swartzwelder, directed by Wesley Archer, aired November 1, 1990, on Fox.

beings behind the processes involved in getting us the food we eat,the clothes we wear, and the homes we live in. Yet James confesses the truth that behind all this is the Father, who is the great gift-giver. Jesus speaks of His Father in the same way, saying, "If you then, who are evil, know how to give good gifts to your children, how much more will your Father who is in heaven give good things to those who ask Him!" (Matthew 7:11).

THANKSGIVING AS RESPONSE TO GOD'S GRACE

Thanksgiving is especially called for through the Scriptures as a response to God's steadfast love, mercy, grace, and kindness. The Psalms show this with the refrain that occurs all over the place in slightly different variations. One such version is as follows: "Oh give thanks to the Lord, for He is good, for His steadfast love endures forever!" (Psalm 106:1). As one of my teachers taught me, whenever you see "for" or "therefore," always ask what it's there for. That little word *for* in the Psalms is very important. It gives the reason, the basis, or the cause for giving thanks. In other words, thanksgiving is the natural response to God's goodness and grace toward us.

In the Greek of the New Testament, this connection is even clearer, as the actual words are linguistically connected. The Greek word commonly translated as "thanksgiving" is *eucharistia.* The word translated as "grace" is *charis.* So, in Greek, the word *grace* is literally embedded within the word *thanksgiving.* You can't miss the connection. Even more striking, the word translated as "joy"—*chara*—is also related linguistically. Grace, thanksgiving, and joy are a package deal in the Christian life. Thus, as Christians, we can see thanksgiving as the joyful response to what God has done for us in Christ.

This focus on God's action in Christ becomes the primary reason for thanksgiving in the New Testament. We see this, for example, in the opening of Paul's epistle to the Christians at Colossae. He tells them:

> **We have not ceased to pray for you, asking that you may be . . . strengthened with all power, according to His glorious might, for all endurance and patience with joy; giving thanks to the Father, who has qualified you to share in the inheritance of the saints in light. He has delivered us from the domain of darkness and transferred us to the kingdom of His beloved Son, in whom we have redemption, the forgiveness of sins. (Colossians 1:9, 11–14)**

We give thanks to God for all His gifts in the realm of creation, but even more do we give thanks for what He has done in the realm of redemption.

OUR TENDENCY TO FORGET

One very simple reason we need to be encouraged over and over to give thanks to God is that we tend to forget. Just as for children, thankfulness does not come naturally to us. We can see this in very simple things, such as the challenge many of us have in writing thank-you notes. At one institution where I studied, the students received a great deal of support from generous donors. The institution wanted to make sure those people were appropriately thanked. However, it could sometimes be difficult to get students to follow through on these tasks, and so the institution endeavored to make it as easy as possible by printing out addressed envelopes and offering templates for thank-you letters. The students were not any more lacking in gratitude than the average person, but they forgot to act on it and express it properly.

This likely brings to mind the famous example of Jesus with the ten lepers. The lepers cry out to Jesus for mercy, and He sends them to the priests. They are cleansed on the way. One returns to praise God and give thanks to Jesus, but Jesus asks, "Were not ten cleansed? Where are the nine?" (Luke 17:17). If even Jesus could receive only 10 percent thanksgiving for a miracle, the problem of forgetful ingratitude would seem quite pronounced.

One very simple reason we need to be encouraged over and over to give thanks to God is that we tend to forget.

The same theme appears in the Old Testament when Moses prepares the people to enter the Promised Land. He says, "When you have eaten and are satisfied, you shall bless the LORD your God for the good land which He has given you. Be careful that you do not forget the LORD your God" (Deuteronomy 8:10–11 NASB). The people had been slaves in Egypt, had wandered through the desert for many years, and were finally coming into the land of plenty. After their many sufferings (often self-inflicted), the Lord's promises were coming to fruition. Moses knew that it was possible to forget all this quite quickly, and so he tried to get out ahead of the problem and warn them against this. Yet forgetful ingratitude was again exactly what happened.

One poet offered a helpful illustration of how we can so easily take things for granted. Consider the beauty of the night sky with the moon, stars, planets, and galaxies, and how few people are out at night looking up at it. The poet suggested that if the night sky were only visible once every thousand years, people would flock to see it and remember it for generations.[21] Yet because it's there every night, we easily forget the beauty and grandeur right outside and rarely take the opportunity to look up. I'm reminded of this myself sometimes. As I write, I am living in the country, so the night sky is even more impressive. When I come home late from a meeting or need to head out into the dark, having forgotten to bring the trash can in, I catch a glimpse of the majesty that is visible above every clear night, and I marvel not only at its beauty but also at how often we seem to forget it.

THANKSGIVING AS PRACTICAL REMEMBRANCE

Thanksgiving in the Bible, then, is encouraged as a way of practically remembering. That specific language is significant. Whereas modern people often talk of gratitude or *feeling* thankful, the Scriptures speak more about *giving* thanks. Thanksgiving needs to be done, not just felt. It's about action, not only sentiment. We know from everyday life that this is what matters most. When a wife shares with her husband that she sometimes feels undervalued and taken for granted, it won't do him much good to respond that he really does feel gratitude for her. She wants to hear it and have it expressed in action. She wants the gratitude to become concrete thanksgiving.

One common way Christians have embedded giving thanks into their lives is through the tradition of meal prayers, often colloquially known as "saying grace." This is an interesting expression, given what we noted earlier about the connection between the Greek words translated as "thanksgiving" and

21 This illustration comes from the 1849 essay "Nature" by the poet Ralph Waldo Emerson.

"grace." A wise Christian mentor once told me that the decline he's noticed in the number of Christian families praying around meals is, to his mind, one of the most drastic illustrations of spiritual ill-health. We don't just write in our journal that we *feel* gratitude for the food and other gifts God gives us; we actually thank Him! As Christian people, we acknowledge that we live in the presence of God. Since all of the good gifts we have in life come from Him, we regularly take some moments before and after meals to give thanks.

Whereas modern people often talk of gratitude or *feeling* thankful, the Scriptures speak more about *giving* thanks.

In this, we follow the example of our Lord Jesus. Consider the famous miracle of Jesus feeding the hungry multitudes who came to Him. Many of us can probably recall the basic details—thousands of people were listening to Jesus teach and became hungry, and Jesus used only five loaves of bread and two fish to miraculously feed the whole crowd, with baskets left over. However, what perhaps is not so firmly entrenched in our memories is what Jesus did between getting the loaves and fish and distributing them:

> **He ordered the crowds to sit down on the grass, and taking the five loaves and the two fish, He looked up to heaven and said a blessing. Then He broke the loaves and gave them to the disciples, and the disciples gave them to the crowds. (MATTHEW 14:19)**

Jesus said grace! He thanked His Father. That simple example can encourage us to do the same.

In the Lutheran tradition, Martin Luther gives one particular way of doing this. He encourages the family to begin with verses from Psalm 145, which fit well with the theme of this book: "The eyes of all *look* to You, and You give them their food in due season. You open Your hand; You satisfy the desire of every living thing" (Psalm 145:15–16, emphasis added). Luther directs families to then pray the Lord's Prayer and this prayer: "Lord God, Heavenly Father, bless us and these Your gifts, which we receive from Your bountiful goodness, through Jesus Christ, our Lord. Amen."[22] Luther suggests a similar pattern for after a meal, using other psalm verses and words for prayer. Many people sit down to eat three times a day. Following Luther's counsel would result in at least six short times of prayer each day that help us not to forget but instead to remember in thanksgiving all that God does for us.

JESUS AND THE LIFE OF THANKSGIVING

I remember speaking to a lady about her Christian life and our congregation. We discussed how many people have drifted away from regular worship and the challenges we faced in encouraging them to gather with their brothers and sisters for Divine Service. The woman expressed that her faith was fairly simple and that she went to church each week, mostly to say thank You to God for all He had given her.

At the time, I wanted to offer a gentle correction. After all, a Lutheran theology of worship focuses on what God does for us rather than what we do for Him. We delight in the reality that Christ is among His people in the Divine Service to serve

22 Small Catechism, Daily Prayers, Asking a Blessing

us through His Word and Sacraments. This is sometimes called the sacramental dimension to worship. Yet what this lady expressed is also important. It is sometimes called the sacrificial side. Thanksgiving is indeed a prominent aspect of our gatherings together, and what's more, Jesus Himself leads us in this thanksgiving to the Father by the Spirit.

Thanksgiving is indeed a prominent aspect of our gatherings together.

Thanksgiving shows up in the Divine Service in various places. We hear it in prayers, hymns, and readings. Yet, most of all, we encounter the call to give thanks in connection with the great thanksgiving Meal of Holy Communion. Another name for this Meal is the Eucharist, which, as we saw earlier, is from the Greek word for giving thanks. As we celebrate the Lord's Supper, Jesus gives us His very own body and blood with the bread and wine. He also hosts this meal and so leads us in thanksgiving to the Father.

We see this in the institution of the Sacrament at the Last Supper itself: "[Jesus] took a cup, and when He had *given thanks* He said . . . And He took bread, and when He had *given thanks*, He broke it and gave it to them" (Luke 22:17, 19, emphasis added). Giving thanks was central to Jesus' institution of His Supper, which is to be regularly celebrated by His disciples until He comes again. The church, therefore, has kept thanksgiving as a central part of our celebrations of the Sacrament. As the pastor calls the people to thank the Lord, they respond that this is fitting and right, and then we often hear words like these: "It is truly good, right, and salutary that we should at all times and in all places give thanks to You, O Lord, holy Father, almighty and everlasting God."[23] The prayer goes on to specify which gifts we are thankful for, often according to the liturgical season.

We do attend worship to receive the good things God gives us. Yet, we also go to church to thank God. And as we look up to Him in thanksgiving for what He has done for us in Christ, even here, we do so only in and through Christ. Our Lord Jesus not only leads us in thanksgiving to the Father, but in the Spirit, He joins us to Himself so that His perfect thanksgiving and our meager thanksgiving are united as one. As Paul puts it, "Whatever you do, in word or deed, do everything in the name of the Lord Jesus, giving thanks to God the Father through Him" (Colossians 3:17).

THANKSGIVING AS ANTIDOTE TO ANXIETY

In the prayer I mentioned above, we speak of thanksgiving as being good and right. In other words, thanking God for all He does for us, especially what He's done for us in Christ, is just the way it should be. Yet we also say (or sing) that it is "salutary." This somewhat archaic word means "giving health." So, while thanksgiving is the right response to God's gifts, it's also good for us. We are more like the human creatures God made us to be when we grow in our life of thanksgiving to God. There is a point of contact here with secular research as well, which has shown that active gratitude or thanksgiving of any sort provides some benefits to our well-being.[24]

---

23 *Lutheran Service Book*, p. 208.

24 See, for example, Lilian Jans-Beken et al., "Gratitude and Health: An Updated Review," *The Journal of Positive Psychology* 15, no. 6 (2020): 743–82, https://doi.org/10.1080/17439760.2019.1651888.

Paul points out one aspect of how thanksgiving can provide godly benefits to us. He presents thanksgiving as an antidote to anxiety. He writes, "Do not be anxious about anything, but in everything by prayer and supplication with thanksgiving let your requests be made known to God" (Philippians 4:6). These are not two unrelated commands—a negative one not to be anxious and a positive one to pray with thanksgiving. Instead, Paul offers an alternative way of life to a problematic pattern of worry and anxiety. The alternative counsel Paul gives is to pray with thanksgiving as a means of combating that problem. Nature abhors a vacuum, and so it's not enough merely to stop doing something. We need to replace it with something positive. Paul wants us to replace anxiety with thanksgiving.

Paul offers an alternative way of life to a problematic pattern.

A very common human worry is about the future and what will happen. When this worry pops up, try thanking God for all the times He's provided for you in the past. Are you anxious about money? Thank God for what you do have. If you worry about a child who has strayed from the life of faith, thank God for their Baptism. In worries at work about how to get done all that you have in front of you, try thanking God for having a job at all. None of this will magically solve the problems we face, but this Spirit-inspired counsel to deal with anxiety through thanksgiving can put things in perspective and help us deal differently with those problems.

Paul himself employed this counsel. We see this in his letters to the early Christian communities. He says at one point that, in addition to his other sufferings, "there is the daily pressure on me of my anxiety for all the churches" (2 Corinthians 11:28).

We can understand this anxiety more clearly when we consider the churches Paul cared for, such as the Corinthian congregation. It's fairly well known that this group of Christians was Paul's problem child, so to speak. The congregation suffered from leadership divisions (1 Corinthians 4), lawsuits between members (1 Corinthians 6), sexual chaos (1 Corinthians 6), drunkenness and other abuses at the Lord's Supper (1 Corinthians 11), and pride and boasting over spiritual gifts (1 Corinthians 14). On top of all this, they challenged the authenticity of Paul's apostleship (2 Corinthians 11).

Yet how does Paul begin his first letter to the Corinthian congregation? He says, "I *give thanks* to my God always for you because of the grace of God that was given you in Christ Jesus" (1 Corinthians 1:4, emphasis added). That's incredible when you know all I've just mentioned above. There were many problems. There was much to worry about and be anxious over at Corinth. Paul gets to that in his letter and has strong words for them at times. Yet he begins by expressing his thanks to God for what He has given these people. According to Paul's own advice, this must have helped him in dealing with the worry they caused him.

A Christian teacher shared a similar story with me. In her early years as a teacher, she had one or two very difficult students in her class. She spent time discussing their attitudes and behaviors with colleagues, and some of that time was simply complaining about how a child could find themselves in such a bad place. One of her fellow teachers encouraged her to pray for the students intentionally

God gave her a new perspective as she spent time in prayer and thanksgiving.

and find reasons to thank God for them—for example, that they were in the school at all and that she had the opportunity to be a positive influence in their lives. The teacher took the advice. To her surprise, she found the problems seemed to shift significantly. In hindsight, she said it wasn't so much that the students dramatically changed but rather that God gave her a new perspective as she spent time in prayer and thanksgiving for those children.

LOOKING UP

Instead of looking inward to solve life's problems, as we are too often encouraged to do, we look up to God in faith to receive His grace, forgiveness, and a new identity as His beloved children. The primary response to those gifts is a different type of looking up—lifting our eyes in joyful thanksgiving for what we have received. It's good and right that we do this, given all that God has done for us, but it's also good *for* us (salutary). This is another significant dimension of being the people God has created—and re-created—us to be. "Give thanks to the Lord, for He is good, for His steadfast love endures forever" (Psalm 136:1).

Reflection Questions

1. What do you remember about your parents teaching you to say thank you?

2. Have you come across secular gratitude journals? What do you think of them?

3. What habits did you have surrounding meal prayers in your family while growing up? What habits do you practice now?

4. Reflect on or discuss the thanksgiving dimension of Divine Service.

5. How do you think thanksgiving can help as an antidote to our worries and anxieties?

CHAPTER 5

LOOKING OUT IN BROTHERLY LOVE

The Christian Community

Let each of you look not only to his own interests, but also to the interests of others.

PHILIPPIANS 2:4

HANGING OUT THE LAUNDRY

I once sat with a man who was reflecting on his many decades of life in the church. He recalled a story from when he and his wife had young children. At the time, life had been somewhat overwhelming. Money had been tight. Work had been busy. The house had been untidy. Looking after small children had been more taxing than either of them had anticipated. At the end of each day, they had both felt exhausted. They were active members of their local congregation, and so there had also been expectations to be involved in various groups, committees, and initiatives. This was over and above regular attendance at worship. Around this time, one of the elders of the congregation had contacted them to arrange a visit to check in.

The man recalled the apprehension he felt ahead of the visit. He had known he wasn't keeping up with life. He would have loved to have been more involved in the church but simply couldn't find the time and energy with everything else that had been going on. They would have also liked to contribute more financially, but their circumstances had made it difficult. He had wondered how the conversation with the church elder would go, given all this.

But none of those fears were realized. The man shared that the elder had not chastised them for their lack of involvement in committees or groups. He hadn't passed judgment on the state of their home. He hadn't asked for money. On the contrary, as the wife had scrambled to attend to a crying child and the husband had fumbled around trying to prepare a cup of coffee, the elder had noticed some clothes in a basket that had come out of the washing machine but had not yet made it outside to the clothesline. So, while he was waiting, he had gone outside and hung out the laundry for them without fuss or ceremony. It was a simple gesture from a fellow Christian. Yet as the man told the story some fifty years later, his eyes still welled up with tears at the impact it had on him. He had experienced the love of the Christian community in a small but tangible way when he had needed it most.

He had experienced the love of the Christian community in a small but tangible way when he had needed it most.

LOVING BROTHERS AND SISTERS

Many of the most intense arguments and fights I remember were with my brothers when we were children. "[Lord,] remember not the sins of my youth" (Psalm 25:7). By the grace of God, we get on well in our adulthood and are, in fact, quite close. Yet in our childhood, things could get rough. A disputed decision in a sports game or infringement onto one's side of the room could result in all-out combat. I'm sure most parents can resonate with seeing this in their children. Sibling tension, rivalry, and conflict are part and parcel of family life. One of the first signs in the Bible of how profoundly sin and evil have impacted God's good creation is in one brother slaying another.

As a parent myself, I see the same squabbles and skirmishes among my own children. Yet on the positive side, I also occasionally get to witness acts of love and kindness between them. When an older sibling voluntarily helps a younger one with homework or with a friend problem at school, the parent's heart melts. Parents are delighted when one child helps clean a sibling's room so they can both enjoy whatever treat is coming. Of course, we want our children to love and serve others outside the family as well. Yet there is a particular kind of joy the parent feels in watching their children act in love for their brother or sister.

Something like this is true for our heavenly Father as we live with one another as brothers and sisters in Christ in the life of the church. While we're called to love any neighbor who crosses our path, even our enemies, the New Testament is also replete with calls specifically to love fellow Christians and cultivate a special kind of community together. This is another important way we respond to God's grace to us in Christ, and

The first people we see when we lift our eyes are the fellow believers who have been redeemed together with us.`

in my schema of looking up and looking out, it is the first way we look out in love. Having looked up to God in faith and thanksgiving, we look out to serve others. The first people we see when we lift our eyes are the fellow believers who have been redeemed together with us.

LOVE ONE ANOTHER

On the night before He died, our Lord Jesus famously gave His disciples a new commandment: "Just as I have loved you, you also are to love one another" (John 13:34). The first part of the command is what makes it new—"just as I have loved you." Jesus tells us to model our love on His. His sacrificial death is both the pattern for this love and the source of its power. On this night, Jesus is also creating a new community and thus offering a new context for this love. Because the disciples are the only people in the room when He speaks this word, "one another" most naturally refers to fellow disciples. This is confirmed by the very next verse, when Jesus says that this love is how all people will come to know that they are His disciples. The love between Christians is a sign to the world of those who belong to Christ. Somewhat mysteriously and even paradoxically, if we are concerned with reaching out to those outside the Christian community, we need to begin by loving those inside it.

This same truth is expressed in various ways by the other New Testament authors. Paul writes, "So then, as we have opportunity, let us do good to everyone, and especially to those who are of the household of faith" (Galatians 6:10). Notice the two truths here. Jesus and the apostles are absolutely clear that we are to show loving kindness to anyone and everyone, regardless of who they are. Yet we also have a special responsibility and obligation toward our fellow Christians. Likewise, John repeats a version of Jesus' new commandment in his letters and often uses the language of "brother," which in the context is most naturally understood as meaning fellow Christians. God has placed us in a new family, with Himself as our Father and other Christians as our siblings. John says that loving fellow Christians is a nonnegotiable element of the Christian life and is linked to our relationship with Christ. Thus, we read, "Whoever says he is in light and hates his brother is still in darkness. Whoever loves his brother abides in the light, and in him there is no cause for stumbling" (1 John 2:9–10).

Loving fellow Christians is a nonnegotiable element of the Christian life.

Sometimes, it can be most difficult to love those closest to us, whether those in our nuclear family—like my brothers and me in the opening example—or in our spiritual family. This is for a variety of reasons. We expect more of one another when we are family. Thus, the failures of family members or fellow Christians hit us harder. We also have a history with these people. We know one another's quirks and foibles. In addition, we are stuck with one another and in it for the long haul. We can't simply encounter one another a few times a year and demonstrate our love through isolated acts of kindness. Instead, love for those close to us requires ongoing patience, forgiveness, and lots and lots of small acts of loving service.

ALONE TOGETHER

I was serving as a parish pastor during the COVID-19 pandemic, and like many congregations, ours decided to begin utilizing technology in a much greater way during that time.

We began by recording sermons, then whole services, and eventually we live streamed. Many blessings came out of this. However, I have had time to reflect and, like many pastors, can see that there have also been downsides. I have spoken to people who have told me straight-out that they loved the live streaming because it meant they could worship God without having to speak to or interact with other people. I was taken aback, to say the least. In other words, one of the unintended consequences of live streaming is that it can, for some, foster and exacerbate the individual dimension of worship at the expense of the communal.

In chapter 1, I introduced the trend of expressive individualism and how pervasive it is not only in Western culture but also in the church. The live streaming example is one way this trend has affected the church, but there are many others. Our congregations can end up existing as a collection of individuals rather than as a whole. However, the New Testament provides a better vision for Christian community, which we'll explore here.

I sometimes tell people that, as hard as it is for prospective pastors and theologians to learn Greek in order to read the New Testament in the original language, I can offer an extremely simple example of why it matters. It's a personal experience to do with one English word: *you*. As someone who has grown up and been formed within an individualistic Western culture, I tend to naturally hear the English pronoun *you* as referring to one person. However, it is ambiguous in English, as the same word is also used to address a group of people. In older forms of English, there were ways of distinguishing the singular and plural second person, and even now, there are some colloquial options, such as the American Southern *y'all*. In Greek, however, there are different words for "you singular" and "you plural."

As I learned Greek, this was my simple but powerful discovery: Many of the instances of "you" in the English New Testament that I had assumed were singular are actually plural. I naturally grew up reading these verses as spoken to *me*, an individual, whereas they are, in fact, spoken to a community.

Let's look at a few examples. Ephesians 2:8–9 says, "For by grace you have been saved through faith. And this is not your own doing; it is the gift of God, not a result of works, so that no one may boast." What do you think—singular or plural? That's right, plural! For by grace *you all together* have been saved through faith. What about this one: "You are the salt of the earth. . . . You are the light of the world" (Matthew 5:13–14). Again, these are plural. You all together as Christian people are salt and light in the world. So often, what we modern Western Christians hear as calls directed to us as individuals are really calls to us as a community. This is not to say that there isn't a very important personal dimension to our Christian life. Yet my sense is that, in our time, we struggle more to embrace the communal dimension.

So often, what we modern Western Christians hear as calls directed to us as individuals are really calls to us as a community.

This communal dimension of the Christian life is fundamentally a gift from God. Christ, the heavenly Bridegroom, loves, cleanses, and sanctifies the church together as His Bride (Ephesians 5:25–26). The Holy Spirit binds Christians together, making them one Body (Ephesians 4:4). God calls and chooses for Himself not just persons but a people (1 Peter 2:10). In the vision of Revelation, the Bride is also the Holy City, new Jerusalem—that is, a community of people who together are forever united with Christ. At the core of Christian community is the work of God, rather than something based only on human activity or interest.

Yet there is also a human contribution to this community. While the life of God's people is established and sustained by His love and Spirit, we are also called to love one another in ways that help cultivate and grow this communal life. This is an example of the proper, active righteousness Luther described. In a right relationship with God, we are purely passive. But we have an active role to play in our relationships with others. It's striking that when Paul gives his famous articulation of the church as the Body of Christ (1 Corinthians 12)—one body with many members who need one another—he immediately follows it with the great chapter on love (1 Corinthians 13). First, there is the description of life in the Body of Christ in all its variety and diversity. Then, there is the call to the sort of attitude and action that will make that Body grow and flourish—namely, the life of love.

This is in stark contrast to a sense of community based mainly on mutual benefit. Often in life, we are together with other people based on what we can get out of it. Yet God calls Christians to cultivate community from the opposite perspective. We do not ask what we can get out of it but rather what we can give and how we can serve. As Paul says, "Let each of you look not only to his own interests, but also to the interests of others" (Philippians 2:4).

LOOKING OUT ON SUNDAY MORNING

The life of worship is fundamental to being a Christian. Jesus and the apostles instructed Christian people to gather to hear God's Word, to confess and be forgiven, to pray, to encourage one another, to gather offerings for the work of God's kingdom, and to celebrate the Lord's Supper. These activities that make up our worship services are communal by nature, especially the Lord's Supper. Sometimes, people claim they can be Christians without going to church. This isn't true, and the simplest response as to why is that you cannot have the Lord's Supper on your own. You must be with at least one other person (a pastor), and ordinarily, with a group of others. So, as we live out our Christian life, we find ourselves regularly gathering with other Christians.

In a previous chapter, I reflected on some of the ways we physically look up to receive God's gifts in the Divine Service and how this is linked to spiritually looking up in faith to God. Now, let's consider that worship setting from another perspective. As you gather with your fellow believers in the Divine Service and look out and around, what do you see?

As you gather with your fellow believers in the Divine Service and look out and around, what do you see?

Look out on a Sunday morning across the people gathered, and you may see people who are rejoicing and people who are weeping. Over there is a mother who is overwhelmed by the needs of a large family, yet over here is a woman who is isolated and lonely. There could be faces you've known for decades and others to whom you can hardly put a name. Look out and you may see rich and poor, successful and struggling, those mature in faith and those still spiritual infants. There is a dear old man, widowed after fifty years of marriage, and the two teenagers who are making eyes at each other across the pews with hope for the future. In most Christian congregations, if you lift your eyes and look around, it will not take long to notice plenty of needs both to pray for and to consider as calls to loving service.

In particular, look out on Sunday morning for the visitors, inquirers, and those who are attempting to come back to church after a long time away. Many established congregations become so comfortable with one another and their routines around Divine Service that they can easily miss the opportunity to love the newcomer in their midst. Many people will tell you that there are few lonelier and more awkward positions than standing by yourself after church, having no one to talk to in a congregation where most people clearly know one another. At one of the congregations where I served as a pastor, there was an older lady who took it as her self-appointed mission to never let this happen. On more than one occasion, I saw her literally chase people down the sidewalk to say hello and invite them back for coffee. Some of the people she "caught" ended up as regulars in our congregation. Having looked up to God in faith and thanksgiving during worship, she was on the lookout for brothers and sisters in need right in our midst.

CHRISTIAN HOSPITALITY

One concrete way this love for fellow Christians can take shape in community is through practices of hospitality. Several places in the New Testament make this connection between love and hospitality quite explicitly. The book of Romans, for example, calls us to "let love be genuine" and then offers several exhortations, including this one: "Contribute to the needs of the saints and seek to show hospitality" (Romans 12:9, 13). Along the same lines, Peter instructs Christians to "keep loving one another earnestly" and to "show hospitality to one another without grumbling" (1 Peter 4:8, 9).

The story of Lydia and her household provides a striking example. As Paul and his missionary companions came to Philippi, they discovered a group of women meeting by the river to pray and proclaimed Christ to them. Amidst whatever else happened in that group, the text focuses on how the Lord opened Lydia's heart to respond in faith. Lydia was a businesswoman, we're told, who dealt in purple cloth. She was seemingly successful, overseeing a whole household that was also baptized together with her. The main point I want to make here, though, is how she responds to this miraculous work of God in her life: "She urged us, saying, 'If you have judged me to be faithful to the Lord, come to my house and stay.' And she prevailed upon us" (Acts 16:15). The Lord opened Lydia's heart; Lydia then opened her home. What's more, we later learn that Lydia's home seems to become a gathering place for Christian believers and an important stopover for the apostles (Acts 16:40), perhaps the beginning of a house church in Philippi.

There are few settings that so naturally facilitate conversation, fun, and community as sitting down over food and drink.

What might Christian hospitality look like for us today? At the most basic level, we are talking about welcoming others into our lives and serving them. Often, we think about this in terms of inviting people to our home for a meal. This is indeed a wonderful way to provide hospitality for one another in the life of the church. The Christian Church is oriented around the Meal instituted for us by Christ. We can then respond in love for brothers and sisters with the meals we prepare. There are few settings that so naturally facilitate conversation, fun, and community as sitting down over food and drink.

Jesus has specific instructions for how we can show hospitality around meals:

> **He said also to the man who had invited Him, "When you give a dinner or a banquet, do not invite your friends or your brothers or your relatives or rich neighbors, lest they also invite you in return and you be repaid. But when you give a feast, invite the poor, the crippled, the lame, the blind, and you will be blessed, because they cannot repay you. For you will be repaid at the resurrection of the just." (Luke 14:12–14)**

It's easier to invite those people whose company we know we will enjoy. It's harder to look out for those who might not have the means to bring a nice bottle of wine, the ability to drive themselves to our home, or the background to engage in polite conversation. Yet love always means looking to the other rather than to ourselves. Look out across your congregation and ask whether there is someone who may have never been invited to a home for a meal before, then consider extending Christ's love in this way.

I'm married with four children, and our family has moved around Australia and has spent time living overseas. Everywhere we've been, we have received beautiful Christian hospitality that has had a big impact on us. As we've moved away from biological family, our children have had surrogate grandparents who have shown them such love. When both my wife and I were graduate students in a foreign land, our local congregation welcomed us and demonstrated this hospitality. I think of one couple who looked out for us in ways we'll never forget, such as taking our whole family out for some lovely meals at places we never would have experienced on our own.

Another strong tradition of hospitality is giving people a place to stay, whether that's for a weekend or much longer. One friend told me of her "host family" in the city where she went to university. This family had taken in dozens of students over the years and provided a Christian welcome for them. It was much more than a bed. They offered a community of faith and love. They took the young people to church. All this had a significant impact on my friend's journey of faith as she met Christian people from outside her family who were willing to take her in and demonstrate Christian love during these formative, and sometimes disorienting, years.

Love always means looking to the other rather than to ourselves.

As I've talked to older members of the congregations I've served, I've often heard stories of when they have stayed at people's homes in connection with church conventions and conferences and when others have stayed with them. I know of people who met future spouses this way or established relationships that have lasted decades. In many circles, people have shifted toward staying in hotels and motels. Although I admit I enjoy some solitude around these big church events, I can't help but wonder whether something profound has been lost when we no longer expect hospitality from our fellow Christians. This is what love does.

There are many challenges, of course, to the practice of hospitality. Many of us feel ill-equipped and overwhelmed by having extra people around our table or in our home. We may worry about the cleanliness of our house or the behavior of our children. Some families are so busy and stressed that they struggle to find time to be together around the table as a family, let alone with others. These and many other concerns are real and not to be minimized. Certain contexts and stages of life may make it easier or harder for people to exercise hospitality.

Yet there are still ways that each of us can welcome and serve our fellow Christians that don't require a spare bedroom or a three-course meal with fine dinnerware. I've known people in those circumstances who intentionally invite someone out for a cup of coffee as their way of exercising hospitality. Others like to walk and invite someone from church to do this with them, and it doesn't cost a cent. Still others look out for those who require help with transportation and offer rides to church or other events. Hospitality need not be grand or expensive in terms of money. What matters is having a heart to welcome others and extending Christ's love to them in whatever ways we can. And the more we practice this, the more we train our eyes to notice and act on these opportunities to build one another up in Christ.

There are still ways that each of us can welcome and serve our fellow Christians that don't require a spare bedroom or a three-course meal.

LOOKING OUT IN LOVE

Our bond as brothers and sisters in the Christian community does not depend on the strength or effectiveness of our love for one another. We are brothers and sisters *in Christ*. He has made it so by reconciling us to Himself and bringing peace. We always look up to Him and His work as the basis of our life together as Christians. As we live together as God's people, the Spirit works in us to foster that community, empowering us to love these brothers and sisters as Christ has loved us. We look not only to our own interests but also to the interests of others. We "bear one another's burdens, and so fulfill the law of Christ" (Galatians 6:2).

Reflection Questions

1. How have you experienced the blessings of Christian community?

2. What impact do you think the culture of individualism has had on the church?

3. Why can it sometimes be hardest to love your fellow Christians?

4. What might it look like for you to "bear one another's burdens" in your local congregation (Galatians 6:2)?

5. What other creative versions of Christian hospitality can you think of?

CHAPTER 6

LOOKING OUT IN NEIGHBORLY LOVE

Service in the World

But a Samaritan, as he journeyed, came to where he was, and when he saw him, he had compassion.

Luke 10:33

SEEING WHAT'S RIGHT AROUND US

A young man recently out of high school was undergoing a time of significant growth in his Christian faith and had a strong desire to serve others. He had embarked on several mission trips overseas with other young people, where he taught English as a second language and helped with other tasks. This seemed worthwhile, and the need was great. Yet he also wrestled with where the Lord was calling him to serve next.

So, the young man talked with a mature Christian person about all this and his feelings of restlessness. The person started asking him simple questions about the needs of his family, his friends, the people who lived on his street, and those who belonged to the local sports club he was in. Were they Christians?

What were their struggles in life? The young man was somewhat embarrassed at how little he actually knew about the needs of these people. He had traveled thousands of miles to serve those he didn't know, yet he hadn't spent much time at all considering how he might serve some of those closest to him. He still thought overseas mission trips could be done in a God-pleasing way, but he was realizing there was a call from God to serve in the relationships he had already been given in his life.

What do we see when we lift our eyes to the wider world around us? Jesus says His disciples are people "not of the world," yet He explicitly prays that we are not taken out of this world but are protected from the evil one as we are sent *into* the world (John 17:14–18). Christians belong to a local church, but they also exist in families, live in neighborhoods, go to school, take up employment, socialize, play sports, have hobbies, volunteer, carry out civic duties, engage in politics, and more. What does it mean for the Christian who has looked up in faith and thanksgiving to God for His grace to now look out in love to serve in those spheres of life?

FINDING DIRECTION BY LOOKING OUT

Consider the difference between the young man I just described and the young woman at the start of the book, who talked with her father about feeling lost, lacking identity and direction. The young woman looked inward and found no stable answers—a crisis of modern life in a culture of expressive individualism. But the young man in this chapter had begun to lift his eyes. Having received his identity as a child of God, he had started to look outward when considering his purpose and direction. Unlike the inward turn of expressive individualism, the Christian faith encourages a person seeking direction in life to look out to what is around them. To be sure, God does apportion among His people varying gifts that can guide how a person directs their life (1 Corinthians 12). Yet when it comes to how we use those gifts, we need to look around at the places we already find ourselves in and consider how God might be calling us to serve others there.

The Christian faith encourages a person seeking direction in life to look out to what is around them.

In another parent-child conversation, this time between a mother and son, the topic came up of how one chooses a course of study or training or a future career. Together, they spoke about what the young man had an aptitude for, and the son also talked quite a bit about where he could make the most money and what he would find fulfilling.

The mother acknowledged the importance of earning a living, especially if he had a family to support one day, and affirmed that people enjoy different types of work. Yet she also wanted to offer an entirely different perspective on the question of a future career, one that stemmed from the family's Christian faith. She encouraged her son not only to consider what would bring self-fulfillment but also to ask what needs were out there in the world that he could meet. Was there a shortage of doctors, nurses, teachers, or tradespeople? That was at least a question he could take into consideration as a Christian. She encouraged him to see his life not primarily for what he could get out of it but for how he could give to and serve others.

THE NEIGHBOR

Jesus' parable of the Good Samaritan is famous for good reason. It has inspired countless people in lives of Christian service, especially toward the poor and needy. Many of us know the story in at least a broad outline. A man is robbed and left for dead. A priest and a Levite pass by him and offer no help. A Samaritan, however, does help the man. He not only attends to the man's immediate needs but also transports him to an inn and pays for his stay. Jesus says the Samaritan is a true neighbor and that His disciples should go and do likewise.[25] I'd like to draw attention to one detail within this well-known story that is linked to the theme of this book.

As each of the travelers passes by, the text emphasizes that they *see* the man in need. In other words, there is no excuse for this lack of compassion on the basis of not noticing the man. The priest and Levite see and purposefully move to the other side of the road to get by. This is surely a dynamic we can all resonate with. If we're in a hurry and see someone a distance away whom we know to be a bit of a talker, we might quickly cross the street to avoid the conversation! Shop owners have been known to request beggars or even people receiving charity donations to move, as their presence might prevent people from walking closer to the shop and stopping in. We know that when we come up close and see a human being in need (or even

25 Although I take Jesus' conclusion at face value—that He calls His disciples to show compassion to those in need as the Samaritan did—I also believe the parable can be read in an allegorical way that understands Jesus as the Good Samaritan helping us in our need. There is a long pedigree to this interpretation in Christian history, going back to figures like St. Augustine.

someone representing them), it is much harder to pass by. This is one reading of the priest's and the Levite's action.

The Samaritan does the opposite. The text says that the Samaritan "went to him" (Luke 10:34). The Samaritan gets a glimpse of something in his peripheral vision that doesn't look good. At that moment, he has a choice: He can keep his eyes straight ahead and ignore what's happening, or he can turn, move toward the problem, and look more closely. That's what he does, and it is when he lays eyes on the person in need—when he truly *looks* at him—that he feels compassion for the man and acts on it. This act of compassion parallels Jesus Himself when He feeds the five thousand. We read in the Gospel of Mark that Jesus "*saw* a great crowd, and He had compassion on them, because they were like sheep without a shepherd" (Mark 6:34, emphasis added).

He can keep his eyes straight ahead and ignore what's happening, or he can turn, move toward the problem, and look more closely.

Jesus is prompted to tell the parable of the Good Samaritan when someone asks, "Who is my neighbor?" (Luke 10:29). That word *neighbor* is significant. It's a case where the etymology matters. *Neighbor* most literally refers to a "near one." We still use it that way; we refer to those who live right beside us as neighbors and use *neighborhood* to signify a group of nearby houses. And while *neighbor* can be understood in a larger sense as "any fellow human being," there is still something important in the parable's detail that the man who fell into the hands of robbers was physically near to those who either passed him or stopped. The man was a "near one," and Jesus asks His hearers to consider who acted as a "near one" to the man in need.

For us, too, looking out in love is both a metaphorical posture for our Christian life as well as a literal part of our service to others. We look out for those God brings across our paths, those who are near to us. We look out for how we can show love and compassion especially to them, no matter who they are.

VOCATION

This leads to an important aspect of Lutheran theology often referred to as vocation. In the wider Christian tradition, this term has been used especially for a calling a person may receive to full-time religious work. However, Luther perceived in his time that the emphasis on priests and those involved in monasticism had devalued the sacred calling of lay Christians in the many areas of life where they spend most of their time. Luther wanted to point out that there, too, Christians were involved in sacred callings to serve the neighbors God had given them.

In Luther's Small Catechism, there is no specific section on vocation. Yet it appears all over as an underlying paradigm. For example, in his explanation of the First Article of the Creed on creation and the explanation of the petition of the Lord's Prayer for daily bread, Luther understands God's work in our daily life to be mediated through other human beings and their work. As a person works as a farmer, truck driver, baker, shop assistant, or any other role, God is at work through them, bringing His gifts. Those people are not working there apart from God but with Him. He is doing His work through them. We see this in Paul's instruction to those who had become Christians in Corinth. Whatever their station or work in life, Paul counseled

Those people are not working there apart from God but with Him.

them to continue serving "in whatever condition each was called" and to remain there "with God" (1 Corinthians 7:24).

Another place we see this underlying theology is in Luther's explanation of confession and absolution in the Small Catechism, where he discusses what sins we should confess. There, he immediately asks people to consider their "place in life according to the Ten Commandments" and then lists various vocations, such as "father, mother, son, daughter, husband, wife, or worker." Then again, in his Table of Duties, Luther offers Bible passages to encourage Christians in their duties and responsibilities in life and organizes them according to various "positions," such as pastors, hearers, those in civil government, and so on. He understands that the life of love, service, and good works varies according to one's vocation.

On this theme of vocation, Luther famously spoke of the God-pleasing work of mothers and fathers tending to crying children and washing diapers, and how God smiles on this sort of work.[26] Luther writes, "What then does Christian faith say to this [service]? It *opens its eyes, looks upon* all these insignificant, distasteful, and despised duties in the Spirit, and is aware that they are all adorned with divine approval as with the costliest gold and jewels."[27] Our faith brings a different perspective to our daily tasks. Faith gives a new set of glasses or brings new vision, so to speak, helping us to see God's calling and pleasure in whatever we do for our neighbor. Through faith, we look out in love.

26 *Luther's Works*, vol. 45, pp. 39–40.

27 *Luther's Works*, vol. 45, p. 39 (emphasis mine).

TRULY SEEING OTHERS

God calls and empowers us to love and serve others—the life of active righteousness, to put it in the language of Luther's two kinds of righteousness paradigm. Consider what your life of active love could look like through the lens of looking out, lifting your eyes to the neighbor in love.

In our previous chapter, we focused on loving fellow Christians, looking out in brotherly love to the family of God. For some, that includes their nuclear family, but that's not the case for everyone. The above quote from Luther reminds us that sometimes our closest neighbors live in the very same house. We should never overlook the needs of our immediate family, the neighbor right in front of us. As you go about your daily routine, beware of becoming so focused on your own tasks that you forget to notice those God has given you to care for, perhaps a spouse, children, siblings, or parents. It's common in our day to observe a family out at a restaurant or in some other social setting, and every person has their eyes down on a screen. We can easily be together and still not *see* one another. Look at the faces of those in your family or household and notice the signs of the burdens they are carrying. There are opportunities there to act in love for them.

Consider the neighborhood or area where you live. My family regularly takes walks out from our home and back. Often, I'm looking around at the trees and birds and mountains off in the distance, taking the opportunity to enjoy the beauty of God's creation. There's nothing wrong with this, of course; Jesus encourages us to do this as a form of meditating on God's provision and alleviating our worry (Matthew 6:25–34). Yet as I walk around my local area, it's also an opportunity to keep my eyes open for needs God brings across my path. As I walk down the street, I notice a house where I used to see a man out fixing his car and recall that he died not too long ago, leaving his wife on her own. I wonder whether she would appreciate a visit or an offer to help around the house. On another corner, there is a man I've often seen sitting in his wheelchair in front of his yard as I've driven by. I've never stopped to talk though. I wonder what he's waiting out there for. What is his story? How might I be called to look out in love to him?

As I walk around my local area, it's also an opportunity to keep my eyes open for needs God brings across my path.

When the newsletter comes home from my children's school or the local sports club, through what sort of lens do I see it? If I'm honest, I usually skim it, trying to glean the minimum amount of information I need so I can get on with other things. Perhaps I could start seeing those communications through the lens of the life of loving service God is calling me to. As I read about the need for reading tutors for some of the children at school, perhaps that's not just a problem for someone else but rather an opportunity for me to look out in love. When the newsletter shares about a family who has just moved to the area from another country, perhaps I can open my eyes to their need for a friendly welcome.

One Christian nurse I know incorporates a literal dimension of looking out in love in her vocation. She works in a secular, public hospital, and she knows firsthand that the health care system is busy and often under-resourced. This means that patients can very easily be reduced to numbers on a chart or tasks to be attended to. She tries to ensure that patients are afforded proper dignity and treated as human beings made in God's image, as people for whom Christ has died. One of the ways she lives this out is through simple eye contact and face-to-face encounters. She makes a point to actually look at people with love and care, taking those few extra moments during her day to catch the person's gaze and communicate that they are valued. Her vocational service to the neighbor finds expression through a powerful type of looking out in love.

SEEING THE HARVEST FIELDS

As well as serving others in love, whatever their human needs may be, Christians also seek to proclaim Christ to all people so that their deepest need is met—peace with God. In the Gospel of John, Jesus uses the language of looking out explicitly in relation to this evangelistic task. He says to the disciples, "Do you not say, 'There are yet four months, then comes the harvest'? *Look*, I tell you, *lift up your eyes*, and see that the fields are white for harvest" (John 4:35, emphasis added). We do well to look out to a world with all sorts of needs and to serve with love where we can. We also do well to look out to this same world and see where there are people who need Christ and His forgiveness. Jesus' words above can encourage us in this. While we often look out to the world and see all those who have drifted away from God and left the church or see people who seem completely closed off to the work of God's Spirit, Jesus sees it differently. He sees in the people who are apart from Him a plentiful spiritual harvest just waiting to be brought in.

A teenage girl attended a school where many of the students and families were not practicing Christians. The principal was always looking for opportunities in school life to bear witness to Christ and invite people to consider the truth claims of the Christian faith and what Christianity looks like in real life. A note came around to several students asking if anyone would consider being on a panel at an assembly to answer questions about their Christian faith and life. The young girl was challenged by this. Any of us who have been to high school know the awkward social dynamics that can accompany such things. She was also a quiet person and not usually inclined to be up in front of people speaking publicly. Yet on this occasion, with the encouragement of others, she decided to volunteer on the panel and proceeded to offer a simple and gentle Christian witness to her peers. She didn't set out to evangelize her friends, but she saw the opportunity presented to her and decided to pursue it with God's help.

Christians also seek to proclaim Christ to all people so that their deepest need is met—peace with God.

An elderly gentleman found himself in a social setting where he was relatively new. As he looked around the room, he saw one younger man who didn't seem to have anyone to talk to and was perhaps a bit out of place. It turned out this man was also new to the area and still meeting folk. The two got to know each other and enjoyed the conversation. The older gentleman, who was an active Christian, didn't come on too strong with spiritual things, yet neither did he hide the fact of his faith when it naturally arose. Several weeks later, the two encountered each other again, and it turned out the younger man was something of a spiritual seeker after many years turned away from God. The older man invited him to a class at his congregation for people wanting to ask questions and learn more. The older gentleman hadn't been on a door-knocking evangelism program. Yet God was at work through him, drawing another lost son to Himself through the man's simple act of seeing the younger man's need and engaging in genuine conversation with him.

LOOKING FOR PRAYERS

Another way Christians love and serve their neighbor is through prayer. As part of His teaching in the Sermon on the Mount, Jesus says:

> **You have heard that it was said, "You shall love your neighbor and hate your enemy." But I say to you, love your enemies and pray for those who persecute you, so that you may be sons of your Father who is in heaven. For He makes His sun rise on the evil and on the good, and sends rain on the just and on the unjust. (Matthew 5:43–45)**

Too quickly, we can hear His instructions to love our enemies and pray for those who persecute us as completely separate things. Certainly, there are many ways one could show love to an enemy. Yet one very natural reading of this verse that is often overlooked is that we can love our enemies and those who persecute us *by* praying for them.[28] And this need not apply only to enemies but also to anyone who comes across our path and who could benefit from our prayers.

We can love our enemies and those who persecute us *by* praying for them.

28 I am indebted for this insight to Dr. John Kleinig. See John Kleinig, *Grace upon Grace: Spirituality for Today* (Concordia Publishing House, 2008), 210–11.

Often, we look out at people in our lives and encounter great and complex issues that can be hard to untangle. We wonder how we are called to love and serve people in situations like these. At times, there is little we can do with our actions to help. Yet, interceding for others and asking that God would intervene in their situations is a means of loving service that is always available to us.

Perhaps in the evening you spend some time in prayer for yourselves and others. Look back over your day in your mind's eye. Whom did you meet? What sorts of encounters did you have? What burdens in people's lives did you discover? It may be that there were opportunities to love and serve these people in those moments or in the context of a longer and ongoing relationship. It may also be that you can best love and serve those people by bringing them to God in prayer and asking for His help on their behalf.

THE PERSISTENCE OF SIN AND NEED FOR WISDOM

As we pursue a life of active righteousness in this world, loving and serving others and giving a reason for the hope we have, we do so in the knowledge that our old sinful nature is always with us. We will always make mistakes and fall short. We'll talk more in the next chapter about this ongoing reality of sin in our lives. To speak of the two kinds of righteousness as Luther did is not to equate them, as if they are the same. The righteousness we have before God on account of Christ is full and perfect. The righteousness we pursue before the world is always partial and tainted by sin in this life. Yet this reality of the two kinds of righteousness is also what gives us confidence to boldly step out into the world to love, serve, and witness where God calls us. Even though we know we will make mistakes, none of that has anything to do with how we stand before God. That question has been settled. God our Father declares us righteous on account of His Son's shed blood. The sins in our life of active righteousness do drive us back to our need for Christ and His grace, but they need not paralyze us into inaction and fear.

Another reality of living in a broken and sinful world is ambiguity. It's not always clear to us what the best decision is, even when we know we want to love and serve. As I go for that walk around my neighborhood, how do I decide whether it's a good idea to visit that widowed lady? As I weigh different needs in my family, school, and workplace, how do I discern where to best use my time and energy? These are real questions that arise constantly in the life of love and service to others. As such, we must also cultivate wisdom in our lives of active righteousness.

It's not always clear to us what the best decision is, even when we know we want to love and serve.

Paul writes to the Romans about this need and how God will grow this wisdom in us through His transformative power:

> **I appeal to you therefore, brothers, by the mercies of God, to present your bodies as a living sacrifice, holy and acceptable to God, which is your spiritual worship. Do not be conformed to this world, but be transformed by the renewal of your mind, that by testing you may discern what is the will of God, what is good and acceptable and perfect. (Romans 12:1–2)**

It's noteworthy that Paul speaks of a need to discern the will of God in the specific circumstances we find in life. In other words, not every occasion and situation in life will have an easy answer spelled out for us as to what God would have us do. We know we are called to love others, even our enemies. We know we are called to serve in the strength God supplies. But what that actually looks like in practice, especially in a world that feels quite confusing for many people, is not always straightforward. We can ask God for the wisdom we need (James 1:5) and "[walk] with the wise" (Proverbs 13:20) in order to grow in wisdom ourselves.

SEEKING DIRECTION

As Christians, we are citizens of heaven (Philippians 3:20), and yet we live in this world. God stations us in all sorts of places in life and is present there with us as we go about our work. Achieving great things in those vocations is not what establishes our righteousness before God. God has already taken care of that in Christ. Neither are our lives in this world simply necessary evils we need to attend to before reaching our heavenly home. Rather, our daily lives in vocation are where we are called as Christians to look out in love and service for our neighbor. This posture can go a long way in providing the direction in life that many people are looking for, in a way that simply can't be found inside ourselves. "Let your eyes look directly forward, and your gaze be straight before you" (Proverbs 4:25).

Reflection Questions

1. Do you think it's true that young people today especially struggle with a finding direction in life? Why or why not?

2. In what ways might the perspective of Christian service impact your consideration of major life decisions?

3. How might the teaching of vocation be helpful for you in your Christian life?

4. What is most difficult for you in your life of Christian service to others?

5. How do you think our actions for others and our prayers for them interrelate?

CHAPTER 7

LOOKING IN RIGHTLY

The Daily Death of the Old Self

Look carefully then how you walk, not as unwise but as wise, making the best use of the time, because the days are evil.

EPHESIANS 5:15–16

LOGS AND SPECKS

A man came to see his new pastor about long-standing problems in the congregation. These were especially between him and some other members. From his perspective, there was unresolved conflict. The man wanted to take the words of Jesus seriously and not simply ignore these issues between brothers and sisters in Christ, who shared in the Lord's Table. The pastor was new to the congregation, so it took the man some time to retell the story of past hurts and sins and for them together to gradually try to untangle the complex set of events that had transpired.

As the pastor listened, he sensed real pain and a genuine desire to make things right. He also perceived that, as is so often the case, the man had a much easier time pointing out the wrongs of the other people than his own shortcomings and faults. The man asked the pastor if he thought it was a good idea to confront the other people about what had happened, lovingly and gently, of course. The pastor affirmed that this was indeed something we are called to do as Christians. It is not good to simply sweep things under the rug. Yet the pastor also encouraged the man to consider another step first. He suggested that the man examine his own conscience and use private confession and absolution for himself before speaking to the other people.

The man took the pastor's advice. On further reflection and self-examination, he could see more clearly how he had contributed to the issues and failed in various ways. He confessed these sins and received absolution. Afterward, the problems he perceived in his congregation didn't go away, but they did look different. He could approach them more realistically, having admitted his own sins and given up on any need to vindicate himself. Here were being lived out Jesus' words in Matthew 7:3–5 about logs and specks, a passage we'll return to later.

LOOKING IN RIGHTLY

I started this book by discussing the problem of looking in, particularly the Western cultural impulse to look inward for identity and purpose. Although the influence of expressive individualism all around us encourages us to answer life's big questions with far too much introspection, we don't need to throw the baby out with the bathwater, as they say. The Scriptures talk about various ways in which Christians engage in introspection. We considered some examples in chapter 1, such as Mary pondering things in her heart. Here, I want to focus on another way of looking in rightly: self-examination.

This type of introspection is part of our life before God and neighbor. Another name for it is mortification, the active putting to death of the old, sinful self. This relates to the striving for holiness in the Christian life and the reality of growth, maturity, and progress. For Luther, this was the daily outworking of our Baptism. Self-examination and the ongoing practice of confession and absolution allow us to look in rightly as we consider our active righteousness toward God and neighbor. Once we know we look up to God in faith to find peace and security, we can rightly look in without fear to reflect on what is getting in the way of our active love of God and neighbor.

This type of introspection is part of our life before God and neighbor.

DAILY DROWNING THE OLD ADAM

In his Small Catechism, Luther poses four main questions to help people learn about God's gift of Baptism. His answer to the fourth question gives us a framework for looking in rightly:

> **What does such baptizing with water indicate? It indicates that the Old Adam in us should by daily contrition and repentance be drowned and die with all sins and evil desires, and that a new man should daily emerge and arise to live before God in righteousness and purity forever.**

While the water is not magical, it does show some of the truth of what happens when it is combined with the Word of God in Baptism. The waters of Baptism drown our old, sinful self. And our Baptism is not a one-off event with no ongoing relevance. On the contrary, Luther says that the water of Baptism points to a daily pattern of life in which the old self is put to death and the new self arises. It's in the practical and specific living out of this counsel that self-examination, or looking in, has its place.

We can only embark on this daily drowning and battle with sin because we are already secure in our life with God, given in Baptism. The Christian person is not engaging in self-examination so that he or she can attain life with God. That has already been established by what God has done in Christ's death and resurrection and given to us in our Baptism. We do not look in at our lives in fear as to how we stand before God; we stand confidently, having looked up in faith to Christ's work for us. Even more than this, the baptized person is united with Christ and indwelled by the Spirit of God. This means we look in and engage in the battle against sin not by our own strength but rather by the Spirit at work in us, forming us into the people God created us to be.

We do not look in at our lives in fear as to how we stand before God; we stand confidently, having looked up in faith to Christ's work for us.

MORTIFICATION

Luther's counsel that the old Adam be daily drowned is linked to the Christian tradition of mortification. This language comes from the New Testament, in which Christians are called to "put to death" or "mortify" various aspects of their sinful life. For example, Paul says in Colossians 3:5, "Put to death therefore what is earthly in you: sexual immorality, impurity, passion, evil desire, and covetousness, which is idolatry." He goes on to connect this language to putting off the old self and putting on the new self (vv. 9–10), language that Luther draws from in his catechism. Paul encourages the Christians at Colossae to do this not in order to become new people in Christ but because they already are. He says they have already died and been raised with Christ. So, one could say, putting to death the sins we commit each day is simply catching up to what God has already done once and for all in Christ.

Romans 8:13 is another place where this theme is picked up. There we read, "For if you live according to the flesh you will die, but if by the Spirit you put to death the deeds of the body, you will live." Important here is the little phrase "by the Spirit," which links to Luther's framing of this within Baptism. We mortify the sinful flesh not by our own strength but by the Spirit's work in us. In other words, mortifying our daily sin cannot be done solely by means of self-discipline or virtuous habits, although these are important. We do it through the very means of the Spirit in God's Word and Sacraments by which God's power is at work in us.

Another part of the scriptural basis here is Jesus' dramatic language in the Sermon on the Mount about gouging out your eyes and cutting off your hands if they cause you to sin (Matthew 5:29–30). We know that the whole reason Jesus came was to die for the sins of the world and bring forgiveness. But forgiveness for sin does not negate the seriousness of ongoing sin and the damage it does in the lives of His disciples, as Jesus' teaching here shows. Until Christ comes again, we live in a state of now and not yet, in which Christ has won definitive victory over sin and yet we continue to struggle with it until we are

Forgiveness for sin does not negate the seriousness of ongoing sin and the damage it does in the lives of His disciples.

made perfect at His return. Thus, Jesus and His apostles consistently counsel that the Christian life includes daily battle against ongoing sin.

SELF-EXAMINATION

So, then, if we are called to daily drown the old Adam, which entails putting to death old sinful habits, attitudes, and practices, how do we actually do that? This is where looking in at our own lives is necessary to know what the problems are for *our* old Adam in particular. Every Christian is called to put to death what is earthly in us, but the specifics will vary from person to person. This process of discerning has often gone by the name of self-examination, and the Ten Commandments have been one of the practical tools used.

We see this in Luther's Small Catechism in his section on confession of sins. Luther says that, while the Christian should plead guilty of all sins before God, "before the pastor we should confess only those sins which we know and feel in our hearts." In other words, Luther sees private confession and absolution as a way to deal with specific sins that burden the individual, something distinct from a general confession of sin to God.

How do we identify these specific sins? Luther points us to the Ten Commandments:

> **Consider your place in life according to the Ten Commandments: Are you a father, mother, son, daughter, husband, wife, or worker? Have you been disobedient, unfaithful, or lazy? Have you been hot-tempered, rude, or quarrelsome? Have you hurt someone by your**

words or deeds? Have you stolen, been negligent, wasted anything, or done any harm?[29]

Here is one way that the daily drowning of the old Adam takes practical and concrete shape in a person's life. This means some self-reflection, looking in at our own lives and examining what's gone wrong for us specifically. Luther reiterates this in his order for confession by leaving space for naming specific sins, saying, "Let the penitent confess whatever else he has done against God's commandments and his own position."[30]

Luther's version of a guide for self-examination is brief but suggestive of a more detailed approach. That is how it has been picked up in the wider Lutheran tradition. Many different and more expansive forms have been developed in which the Ten Commandments are used as a mirror for self-examination, especially before confession and absolution. This, I suggest, is a right way to look in as we examine our own conscience. The light of God's Word and the work of His Spirit help us to look in and see the true depth of our sin, not so we can dwell on it incessantly but so we can confess it and have it dealt with again by God's word of forgiveness.

The Ten Commandments are used as a mirror for self-examination.

PRIVATE CONFESSION

I'll never forget my first experience of this sort of self-examination and the impact it had on my Christian life. At the

29 Small Catechism, Confession, How Christians Should Be Taught to Confess.

30 Small Catechism, Confession, A Short Form of Confession.

Lutheran school I attended, confirmation instruction was embedded within class time and led by the congregational pastor. Toward the end of our program, we were all expected to use private confession and absolution with the pastor. I sometimes tell young people that Luther said no one should be compelled to go to confession, but I was compelled, and I'll be forever grateful for it! As I sat outside awaiting my turn, I watched some of the other young people leave, obviously quite moved by the experience. I had no idea what I was going to say or how to handle it once I got in there.

My turn came, and I nervously entered. When it came time to name any specific sins that weighed on me, I went blank. I certainly knew in general I was a sinner, but when it came to specifics, I found it difficult to pin down and name any. The pastor then started gently leading me through a version of Luther's counsel on the Ten Commandments and our position in life tailored to me. He asked me to consider things like my attitude, words, and actions toward my parents and siblings. He got me to reflect on my life as a student. Fairly soon, the mirror of God's holy Law, expressed especially in the Ten Commandments, together with God's Spirit, did its work. I could name the specific sins I felt in my heart, and I received the liberating and powerful word of forgiveness and peace.

This practice of looking in at one's life according to the Ten Commandments is very helpful before using private confession with a pastor. The habit of self-examination can also be profitable before worship, perhaps on Saturday night before bed, especially since in the modern church we nearly always have a public confession and absolution as part of the Divine Service. More widely than this still, parts of the Christian tradition have encouraged versions of this each night before bed. As we pray the Lord's Prayer and ask for God's forgiveness as we forgive others, some brief reflection in connection with this can add a helpful specificity. We might look back over our day and the interactions we've had and reflect on our thoughts, words, and actions in light of God's Ten Commandments. We do this not to punish or aggravate ourselves—quite the opposite. Our generic sense of unease in conscience can be spiritually clarified, and we rest in the knowledge of God's forgiveness and peace that is ours each day in Christ.

We might look back over our day and the interactions we've had and reflect on our thoughts, words, and actions in light of God's Ten Commandments.

FASTING

Another discipline that prepares us for our ongoing battle against sin is fasting. Like self-examination, fasting can help us look in rightly and see our sin more clearly, all to prepare us for the word of forgiveness in Christ.

Fasting is mentioned in many places in the Scriptures. Often, it is described as an activity carried out by the people of God that relates to repentance or prayer. Jesus Himself fasted in connection with His temptation by the devil, and He cautioned His disciples about fasting in the right way—namely, not doing it as a show for others. Elsewhere in the New Testament, Scripture refers to various other individuals or communities who fasted in their Christian piety or ministry. Throughout Christian history, fasting has been a normal practice in one form or another, although it has been far less utilized in modern times.

Paul's words in 1 Corinthians about discipline and control in the Christian life are often linked to fasting. While Paul does not mention it explicitly, fasting has long been understood as one form of discipline that develops self-control:

> **Every athlete exercises self-control in all things. They do it to receive a perishable wreath, but we an imperishable. So I do not run aimlessly; I do not box as one beating the air. But I discipline my body and keep it under control, lest after preaching to others I myself should be disqualified. (1 Corinthians 9:25–27)**

Most people resonate with the analogy of an athlete. Athletes alter their diets to fuel performance, get up early to practice, and work out to train their bodies. When it comes to the big event and they feel like slowing down or giving up, the work they've done in training bears fruit. So it is, Paul says, with the spiritual life. Our sinful flesh tempts us toward certain things. Discerning, confessing, and being forgiven of these sins is most important. But in the ongoing struggle, it can be helpful for Christians to train their bodily desires by denying themselves certain things for a period of time. This is fasting.

Historically, Christians have had certain days or times of the week when they've regularly fasted. The season of Lent, for example, is often a time when Christians take up fasting as a form of Christian discipline. We might fast from alcohol or from food at certain periods on some days of the week. Modern Christians have increasingly been fasting from forms of technology and social media. We do this not so much to please God (although in Matthew 6, Jesus encourages us that the Father sees these acts of piety and rewards us) but in order to train our bodies in the ongoing struggle against sin in this life.

Fasting also relates to our life of love. As one friend of mine likes to note, it's more difficult to love people when you're hungry! Suddenly, we discover how weak our flesh really is when just a day or two of abstaining from food or drink makes us impatient with those around us. Our love for others is also under training, in a sense, as we learn to do it under fasting conditions.

We do this . . . in order to train our bodies in the ongoing struggle against sin in this life.

LOOKING IN TO LOOK UP

We can also practice looking in rightly as we prepare for the Lord's Supper. In fact, the New Testament specifically links self-examination to the reception of the Lord's Supper. After handing on the words of institution and warning against eating and drinking in an unworthy manner and so being "guilty concerning the body and blood of the Lord," Paul says, "Let a person examine himself, then, and so eat of the bread and drink of the cup" (1 Corinthians 11:27–28). There are specific issues going on in Corinth to do with their conduct at the Supper and how they are treating one another in the life of the congregation. However, Christians have also taken this in a broader sense as encouragement to a general self-examination as part of a right reception of the Lord's Supper.

Luther likewise includes a form of self-examination in his questions and answers prepared for those who intend to go to the Sacrament. The first question is "Do you believe that you are a sinner?" to which the answer is expected to be an emphatic yes. The second question is "How do you know this?" to which the answer is "From the Ten Commandments, which I have not kept." In other words, as Luther sought to prepare people to receive the body and blood of Christ in the Sacrament, he presupposed some sort of self-examination using the Ten Commandments, similar to what he laid out in the short order of confession.

As we consider this ongoing life of the old self being drowned daily and sins being put to death—a pattern that requires an element of looking in—we could say that this happens within the framework of Baptism and the Lord's Supper. Our Baptism into Christ means that we battle against sin as those who have already been forgiven and received into God's family as beloved children, and the Lord's Supper is Christ's ongoing application of this forgiveness and a source of power in the battle. These external means of God's grace and Spirit prevent our looking in at our own sin from becoming a downward spiral of introspective despair. Even as we look in, we do so in order to look up again in faith to God's grace to us in Christ.

These external means of God's grace and Spirit prevent our looking in at our own sin from becoming a downward spiral of introspective despair.

LOOKING IN TO LOOK OUT

There's also a sense in which we look in at our sin in order to better look out to our neighbor in love. Luther picks up on this when he discusses mortifying our sin. Looking again at Luther's order of confession, for example, we see that he encourages Christians to confess not only what we have done against God's commandments but also what we have done against our own "position"—that is, against our vocations. Luther encourages Christians to reflect on their sins especially in relation to their callings in life, so that in identifying sins there, repenting, and being forgiven of them, we can be sent back into those very vocations in order to love and serve where God has placed us.

Jesus Himself offers a dramatic image of the need to see ourselves and our own sin clearly as we interact with others:

> **Why do you see the speck that is in your brother's eye, but do not notice the log that is in your own eye? Or how can you say to your brother, "Let me take the speck out of your eye," when there is the log in your own eye? You hypocrite, first take the log out of your own eye, and then you will see clearly to take the speck out of your brother's eye. (Matthew 7:3–5)**

Picture it: a person walking around with a giant log sticking out of their eye while they call attention to a speck of dust in another person's eye. This is Jesus' analogy for those who want to confront and correct others but have not seriously examined their own sin. Like the man in the opening story of our chapter, we do well to follow Jesus' advice and humbly examine ourselves before attempting to examine others.

Jesus does not teach people to take the log out of their own eye and leave it at that.

Yet this is one of those cases where the first part of what Jesus says is so striking that we can miss the conclusion. Jesus does not teach people to take the log out of their own eye and leave it at that. Neither does He say that once we remove our own log, we'll actually discover there was no speck there in the other person's eye after all. Instead, He teaches that after we remove our own log—which I'm suggesting can happen through self-examination, confession, and absolution—we will have clearer spiritual sight to see the speck for what it really is. He even says our clearer sight will enable us to help the other person with their speck. So, we look in at our own shortcomings and failures, but then we lift our eyes again, now better able to see how we can love and serve those around us.

LOOKING IN FOR SPIRITUAL GROWTH

In this book, I have offered a significant critique of and caution against the modern tendency to look inward, especially for answers to life's big questions. It's for this reason also that I've left this attempt to articulate a proper place for looking in much later in the book. Regardless of the cultural context we find ourselves in though, there is still a proper place for inwardness, introspection, and looking in. Christians can especially look in by self-examination of conscience. We do this not to discover who we truly are or how we stand before God, as this is only ever given to us as a gift from outside ourselves. Rather, we look in to gain spiritual clarity about our lives before God and others and to grow in our life of love. "Let us test and examine our ways, and return to the LORD!" (Lamentations 3:40).

Reflection Questions

1. Have you experienced practices of self-examination in your Christian life? In what ways were they helpful? How can they be misused?

2. Have you used private confession and absolution with a pastor before? Why do you think this is difficult for many people to imagine doing?

3. Are you familiar with the Christian tradition of mortification of sin? Why do you think this language isn't used as much in our times?

4. How has fasting been a part of your Christian life? What makes this challenging today?

5. What have you found to be helpful preparations for receiving the Lord's Supper?

CHAPTER 8

LOOKING FORWARD IN HOPE

The Anticipation

For he was looking forward to the city that has foundations, whose designer and builder is God.

Hebrews 11:10

ANTICIPATION

I remember days from my youth when we were expecting family or friends to visit on a weekend or holiday. It was exciting, as I knew there were fun times to be had with cousins or close friends, catching up and playing games. The arrival of our visitors would also bring that festive and relaxed mood to the household, where normal routines were suddenly suspended. Likely, there would be pizza or other take-out food for dinner. If it was summer, we could spend hours outside late, playing as our parents talked inside or on the porch.

Often our guests were traveling from quite a distance, so we wouldn't necessarily know when they were arriving. There were some preparations to be made for our visitors—and no doubt we could've helped much more than we did as children! There was also a sense in which the hours leading up to their arrival proceeded with the regular activities we might be doing on any other day. Yet, it all felt different because of the anticipation of our visitors. As I read a book, rode my bike, helped my parents, or tidied my room, I went about it with one eye on the road and the driveway, where I knew the car would soon be rolling in. I was looking forward to something joyful on the horizon of my day, and that anticipation changed my experience of the time leading up to the big event.

It all felt different because of the anticipation of our visitors.

The New Testament brims with the joyful expectation of Christ's coming again in glory. As Christians, we live in this world with one eye on the horizon of history, so to speak, looking forward in anticipation of the One who will return in the same way the disciples saw Him go (Acts 1:11). This is a looking forward in hope, even as we now look up to God in faith and out to our neighbor in love. In this chapter, we return to the opening reflections of our introduction and what was, in many ways, the inspiration for this book, the final phrase of the Nicene Creed. There we confess our belief in the Holy Trinity and the tenets of the faith and finish by saying, "[We] look for the resurrection of the dead and the life of the world to come."

HEARTS WEIGHED DOWN IN AN IMMANENT FRAME

We need to keep confessing and cultivating this posture of lifting our eyes in hope to God's fulfillment of His promises because the world around us and our own sinful flesh constantly try to eclipse this hope. In part 1 of this book, we discussed

Charles Taylor's notion of the immanent frame. One way this has especially influenced Christianity is that the more transcendent dimensions of the faith have sometimes receded into the background of our worldview. The promised return of Christ in glory for final judgment and the resurrection of all people is one of these dimensions.

In other words, in the modern world, it is sometimes easier for Christians to talk about how their belief in God brings meaning to this life or provides a moral framework for how we live than to discuss the reality that Christ promises to come again and renew all things (Matthew 19:28). It's possible that certain periods of church history or subcultures of the church today have the reverse problem, in which there is a nearly exclusive focus on the otherworldly. Yet overall, the modern Western world tends to block our view of this future horizon and trap us within the here and now.

Another major reason this aspect of our faith can fade from view is because our own sinful flesh encloses us within little worlds of our own making. Jesus warns repeatedly about this, saying, for example, "Watch yourselves lest your hearts be weighed down with dissipation and drunkenness and cares of this life, and that day come upon you suddenly like a trap" (Luke 21:34). It can be our own sins or the response of our sinful flesh to the many anxieties this life can bring that weigh our hearts down and cause us to fall into spiritual drowsiness. Jesus' parable of the wise and faithful servant makes this same point. The writers of the New Testament call us to a hopeful and

The writers of the New Testament call us to a hopeful and expectant anticipation of Christ's return in glory.

expectant anticipation of Christ's return in glory, even as, and perhaps especially because, they also know all that works against this posture both around and within us.

LOOKING IN EXPECTATION

In the introduction to this book, I drew attention to the word *look* in the last sentence of the Nicene Creed: "[We] look for the resurrection of the dead and the life of the world to come." This part of the Christian faith considers what are sometimes called the "last things," or eschatology, to use the more technical word. So, when it comes to the last things, why did those in the early church land on that word *look*? The Greek word in the original version of the Creed, *prosdokaō*, is used in the New Testament specifically in relation to the expectation of the Messiah and of the last things more generally. It can be translated as "look for," "wait," or "expect." Another New Testament word, *prosdechomai*, is commonly translated in very similar ways. This word is used at other key places in relation to eschatological themes. Together, it seems these sorts of uses form the background for the Creed's phrase. It's worth noting a few of these key places as we meditate on the theme of looking forward in hope and anticipation.

When Mary and Joseph present Jesus in the temple, the writers describe the faithfulness of both Simeon and Anna as a looking forward. Simeon is righteous and devout, and one of the main things this means in the context is that he is "looking forward to the consolation of Israel" (Luke 2:25 NASB). After Simeon's words to Mary and Joseph, Anna arrives, giving thanks to God and speaking about Jesus to all the others "who were looking forward to the redemption of Jerusalem" (Luke 2:38 NASB).

John the Baptist sends word to Jesus, asking if He is, in fact, the Messiah they have been waiting for, saying, "Are You the one who is to come, or shall we look for another?" (Matthew 11:3). At the burial of Jesus, Joseph of Arimathea is described in a way similar to Simeon and Anna, as one who is "looking for the kingdom of God" (Luke 23:51). So, in the Bible, looking forward in anticipation can have a general sense of expectation and longing for God to bring about what He has promised. For the saints of old, this especially meant the promise of the coming of the Messiah.

Looking forward in anticipation can have a general sense of expectation and longing for God to bring about what He has promised.

In Jesus' own teaching, He uses the language of looking for the expectation of His coming again in glory, a use followed by later New Testament writers. In a parable that speaks about His return, Jesus says, "The master of that servant will come on a day when he is not looking for him and at an hour that he is not aware of" (Matthew 24:50 NKJV). Paul writes to Titus and describes how Christian people are to be "looking for the blessed hope and the appearing of the glory of our great God and Savior, Christ Jesus" (Titus 2:13 NASB). Jude encourages the recipients of his letter to keep building themselves up in their most holy faith, praying in the Spirit, keeping themselves in the love of God, all while "looking forward to the mercy of our Lord Jesus Christ to eternal life" (Jude 21 NASB). This is all built on the promise of Jesus that He will come again (e.g., John 14:3), a promise reiterated by the angels at His ascension that He "will come in the same way as you saw Him go" (Acts 1:11).

Peter's second letter is arguably the clearest biblical background for the Creed's phrase. The same word used in the Nicene Creed is used three times in the space of several verses in relation to the promise of new heavens and a new earth. Let's note the larger section here:

> **But the day of the Lord will come like a thief, in which the heavens will pass away with a roar and the elements will be destroyed with intense heat, and the earth and its works will be discovered. Since all these things are to be destroyed in this way, what sort of people ought you to be in holy conduct and godliness, *looking for* and hastening the coming of the day of God, because of which the heavens will be destroyed by burning, and the elements will melt with intense heat! But according to His promise we are *looking for* new heavens and a new earth, in which righteousness dwells. Therefore, beloved, since you *look for* these things, be diligent to be found spotless and blameless by Him, at peace, and regard the patience of our Lord as salvation. (2 Peter 3:10–15 NASB, emphasis added)**

It's worth noting here the connection between this forward-looking hope Christian people have and the life of holiness we live now. One concern people sometimes have about too much focus on the life of the world to come is that it may somehow cause us to disdain this life, this world, and the people around us. Yet in the New Testament, the hope we have for the future is consistently given as a reason, basis, or cause for the life we live now.

LOOK TO THE EAST!

In *The Lord of the Rings* movies, the character Gandalf needs to leave his compatriots as they prepare to do battle. He promises to return at a crucial time, though, and bring the assistance they will need. He tells them that at dawn on the fifth day, they should "look to the east." Amid exhaustion, imminent defeat, and seeming hopelessness, they are to look toward the horizon where the light dawns. That is where they will find hope. And indeed, Gandalf is true to his promise and arrives with the help they need just when all seems lost. The biblical theme of looking forward in hope runs throughout *The Lord of the Rings* and can remind Christians of the hope we have in Christ, especially the hope of His return in glory.

Jesus said, "For as the lightning comes from the east and shines as far as the west, so will be the coming of the Son of Man" (Matthew 24:27). From early in the life of the church, Christians often built churches facing east in acknowledgment that Christ is the light of the world and that, at least symbolically, we look to the east for the hope of His glorious return. This dimension of church history is by no means essential, but it is lost on many Christians today. We do well to remember that our forebearers in the faith saw fit to have a reminder of our hope in Christ's return and final redemption literally built into the life of the church.

Our forebearers in the faith saw fit to have a reminder of our hope in Christ's return and final redemption literally built into the life of the church.

Whether the church buildings face east is one thing, and certainly a person can maintain true Christian hope whether they know their east and west or not! Another part of this legacy, though, is structuring our worship spaces so that the congregation all faces the same direction. Again, this need not always be the case, and there are examples early in church history of churches in various shapes, including being in the round. However, when a congregation all faces one direction—usually toward an altar, where God is present with His people in Word and Sacrament—Christians have traditionally understood this as facing east symbolically, no matter what direction it is literally. Here, in the way many Christians have traditionally arranged themselves for worship, is an orientation that reminds us of our forward-looking, hope-filled posture in this life.

FAITH, HOPE, AND LOVE

Earlier in this book, I laid out some of the theological framework behind lifting our eyes to look up and out. This was to do with Luther's paradigm called the two kinds of righteousness, which I argued is closely related to the biblical pair of faith and love. Now, however, as we near the end of this book and consider the importance of looking forward in anticipation to the future God has for us, we do well to recall the third virtue that often accompanies faith and love in the New Testament: hope.

Most famously, Paul speaks of the triad of faith, hope, and love in 1 Corinthians 13:13, where he says, "The greatest of these is love." His point is that while we live by faith and look forward in hope in this life, those things will have become redundant in the life to come, when we will see God face to face. But love will remain even there, permeating the community of heaven. Elsewhere, Paul mentions the three together in a particularly interesting relationship. He writes to the Colossians, "We always thank God, the Father of our Lord Jesus Christ, when we pray for you, since we heard of your *faith* in Christ Jesus and of the *love* that you have for all the saints, because of the *hope* laid up for you in heaven" (Colossians 1:3–5, emphasis added). In this formulation, hope is something of the basis for faith and love.

This formulation in Colossians gives hope a priority of sorts, saying that our faith and love follow from our hope.

While the creedal flow of thought locates hope toward the end, as I have done in this book, this formulation in Colossians gives hope a priority of sorts, saying that our faith and love follow from our hope. One commentator describes the relationship in the following imaginative way:

> **Faith is the soil from which the fruit of love springs, and hope is the sunshine which ripens this fruit of love. By faith Christ unites all believers so that, joined thus, they love each other; Christ has laid away the treasure of hope in heaven for all believers so that, united by the hope of this expected treasure, we for this reason also love each other.**[31]

The person who has Christian hope as the "anchor of the soul" (Hebrews 6:19) will live by faith and love in this life.

GRAVES AND RESURRECTION

As we come to that final line of the Nicene Creed, we confess that we look forward not to a vague notion of the afterlife or the immortality of the soul but to the *resurrection* of the dead. The

31 R. C. H. Lenski, *Interpretation of Colossians, Thessalonians, Timothy, Titus, Philemon* (Wartburg Press, 1946), 23.

Apostles' Creed is even more explicit in saying the resurrection of the *body*. It's for this reason that our Christian hope manifests in such a profound way at the time of funerals, and even more so at graveside committals. In modern Western culture, these dimensions of the funeral have been diminished as the focus shifts toward remembering and celebrating the deceased's life. Often, a graveside service is now considered too much fuss, and sometimes even the body and coffin are elsewhere at a funeral while mourners pay their respects.

Christians, though, need not avoid facing the reality of death. We have the dead body in a coffin in the church, and we stand next to that body and proclaim, "In the sure hope of the resurrection of the dead and the life of the world to come, we take the body of our brother/sister in Christ to its lasting resting place." From a human point of view, this is an outrageous claim. Yet faith in Christ's finished work and the firstfruits of His resurrection give His people a sure and certain hope. I believe Christians should make attendance at funerals a priority when possible, joining fellow Christians in boldly declaring our hope in the face of death. And we should take our kids too. This is a point at which the liturgy will teach and form the people of God in the posture of looking forward in hope.

In my own experience, the committal at the graveside is even more striking in this respect. There, not only do we have a deceased person in our presence, but we lower that body into the ground. We even acknowledge in a profound way the just judgment of God on our sin, the sting of death, and the reality of decay in this fallen world as we say, "Ashes to ashes, dust to dust; dust we are, and to dust we shall return." However, as we lower a body into the ground, a body we know will decay (unless the Lord returns soon), even there we boldly, defiantly confess our hope in Christ, who says, "I am the resurrection and the life. Whoever believes in Me, though he die, yet shall he live, and everyone who lives and believes in Me shall never die" (John 11:25–26). Amen!

As we lower a body into the ground, . . . even there we boldly, defiantly confess our hope in Christ.

In an earlier chapter, I wrote about my experience as a pastor when people look up during key moments of the Divine Service to hear the Gospel promises and declarations to them. The same thing happens, perhaps even more so, during confessions of Christian hope at funerals. It's a truism among clergy that weddings are more challenging to conduct than funerals. At weddings, many pastors have the experience of noting very few ears and eyes attentive to the Word of God. Sometimes, even the couple is distracted—understandably, perhaps, on their big day! Yet at funerals, it's often the opposite. People are confronted with the reality of death, separation from their loved one, and their own mortality. Christian believers look expectantly to the messenger of Christ to deliver to them the comfort of God's word of hope, and even those who do not regularly attend worship often have ears open. They look up to hear how they, too, can confidently look forward.

LOOKING FORWARD IN SUFFERING

Another way the New Testament touches on the theme of looking forward in hope is in relation to suffering. We can be encouraged during suffering and drawn through it by God's grace in Christ as we look forward to the fulfillment of His promises. This is articulated most clearly in Paul's second letter to the Corinthians, in what is also a profound instance of a spirituality of looking, which I've been reflecting on throughout this book. About suffering, Paul says:

> **For this light momentary affliction is preparing for us an eternal weight of glory beyond all comparison, as we look not to the things that are seen but to the things that are unseen. For the things that are seen are transient, but the things that are unseen are eternal.** (2 Corinthians 4:17–18)

There is something paradoxical and mysterious about Paul's words here. How does one look to something that cannot be seen? We cannot literally look to what is unseen, but we direct the eyes of our heart toward those things that reside in the unseen realm of God and the angels. Paul's reasoning is straightforward. What you can see will not last forever, so don't focus on that. What you can't see—namely, God and the spiritual blessings He has in store for you—will last forever, so focus on that. And here's the big point: We do this amid what he calls our "light momentary affliction." In other words, as we journey through life and face disappointment, pain, disease, betrayal, hostility, depression, conflict, and so much more, those things do not need to be all we can see. Instead, we look to the things beyond, in God's realm, and receive His help for all we encounter in this life.

We look to the things beyond, in God's realm, and receive His help for all we encounter in this life.

As we discuss suffering, hope, the seen, and the unseen, I can't help but think of the story of American hymn writer

Fanny Jane Crosby. Although Lutherans wouldn't commonly use most of her hymns, her story is inspiring. Crosby was a prolific hymn writer in the revivalist tradition, despite being blind from infancy. When one is aware of the challenges she faced in life, it's striking to note how the themes of future glory and the vision of Christ show up in her hymns. For example, in the hymn "Blessed Assurance," about the blessing of salvation in Christ, Crosby writes: "Visions of rapture now burst on my sight. Angels descending bring from above echoes of mercy, whispers of love" (st. 2). In the hymn "To God Be the Glory," she writes, "But purer, and higher, and greater will be our wonder, our transport, when Jesus we see" (st. 3). Through her suffering, she looked forward in faith and hope to what was unseen, longing for the day she would see Jesus face to face (1 John 3:2).

SINGING OUR HOPE

This leads me to mention the place of hymnody more generally as a way in which the saints who have gone before us have helped to ensure that Christians do not stop looking forward in hope. For me, this eschatological dimension of my faith has grown and been enriched as I've learned and appreciated the hymns to do with the end times, the church triumphant, resurrection and judgment, and the life everlasting. As we sing these hymns, it's hard to miss the fact that they have been written from deep meditation on the words and themes of Scripture, as well as being a realistic facing up to one's own mortality. Many of these hymn writers had personal experience with pervasive human tragedies like war and plague. When one compares many contemporary, folksy Christian songs with these hymns of previous centuries, the contrast is stark. Countless songs we have sung at youth groups and around campfires are fine as far as they go, but one is hard-pressed to find a song among them that would be fitting to sing at a funeral or graveside, let alone during a plague or war.

Let's consider a few examples. If you want to feel the solemn scriptural teaching on the end times, you won't regret learning "The Day Is Surely Drawing Near."[32] It captures the severity with which the Scriptures describe aspects of the final judgment, but also how the believer finds refuge in Christ and His work. It speaks of when "we shall see Him face to face, with all His saints in that blest place" and finishes by praying, "O Jesus Christ, do not delay."

If you want to capture the joy of the church as the Bride meeting her heavenly Bridegroom when He comes, it's hard to do better than singing "Wake, Awake, for Night Is Flying."[33] This is one of those hymns where the tune matches the words in a profound way. It again picks up these themes of vision as it speaks of how "no eye has seen the light, no ear has heard the might of Thy glory." It's pointing to that unseen realm that we look to now by faith but one day will truly see.

We can sing the hope we have in Christ into our hearts and into the hearts of one another.

If the promises of the life of the world to come seem distant and removed from the cares of everyday life, join with Christians since the twelfth century in the hymn "Jerusalem the Golden."[34] This is one of my personal favorites. I only recall learning to sing it well into my adulthood and remember

32 *Lutheran Service Book* 508:6, 7.

33 *Lutheran Service Book* 516:3.

34 *Lutheran Service Book* 672.

wondering where this hymn had been all my life. Among many other images, the hymn draws on the language of Hebrews 11 and how the saints of old desired "a better country, that is, a heavenly one" (Hebrews 11:16). For C. S. Lewis fans, these lines may evoke the themes of Aslan's country in Narnia. Further up and further in!

Paul reminds us that we should be "teaching and admonishing one another in all wisdom, singing psalms and hymns and spiritual songs" (Colossians 3:16). The hymns that lift our eyes to our Christian hope are an especially powerful resource in this connection. We can sing the hope we have in Christ into our hearts and into the hearts of one another.

FORETASTE OF THE FEAST TO COME

In our chapter on looking up in faith, I spent some time on the Lord's Supper. There our gracious Lord comes to dwell with us in His body and blood with the bread and wine. We kneel before the altar with open hands and mouths, looking up in faith to receive Christ and His gifts of forgiveness, life, and salvation in the present. We also do well, though, to pay attention to the eschatological dimension of the Lord's Supper. In this Holy Meal, we "proclaim the Lord's death until He comes" (1 Corinthians 11:26). We look forward in hope to the One who will come again in glory, even as He came once in the flesh, and comes to us now in the Sacrament.

In the Lutheran tradition, the liturgy surrounding Communion confesses this truth in several ways. After the words of institution, the pastor speaks the words from 1 Corinthians 11:26, saying, "As often as we eat this bread and drink this cup, we proclaim the Lord's death until He comes." The congregation responds with a prayer drawn from the cry of the saints in Revelation 22:20: "Amen. Come, Lord Jesus."[35] One of the post-Communion collects speaks of God giving us "a foretaste of the feast to come in the Holy Supper."[36] More widely in the liturgy, the hymn of praise "This Is the Feast" expresses this same truth.[37] All this recalls the many biblical depictions of eternal life with the triune God as a feast, such as in Isaiah 25:6–9; Psalm 23:5–6; and Revelation 19:6–9. As Jesus celebrates the Last Supper with His disciples and prepares for His Passion, He says, "And I assign to you, as My Father assigned to Me, a kingdom, that you may eat and drink at My table in My kingdom and sit on thrones judging the twelve tribes of Israel" (Luke 22:29–30).

Arthur Just writes about all this in some depth, noting how "the experience of the last things has already begun in our worship! This is what some call 'inaugurated eschatology.'"[38] His concern is especially for Christians to be aware of how the future realities of heaven become present for us in the here and now. This is a wonderful mystery and one that brings great comfort and joy for the Christian. But the traffic goes both ways, so to speak, in this dynamic. Even as we are comforted in the present by the presence of heaven on earth in the Sacrament,

We are propelled forward in hope as our earthly celebration already participates in the future glory that will one day be ours.

35 *Lutheran Service Book*, p .179.

36 *Lutheran Service Book*, p. 183.

37 *Lutheran Service Book*, pp. 171–72.

38 Arthur A. Just Jr., *Heaven on Earth: The Gifts of Christ in the Divine Service* (Concordia Publishing House, 2008), 19–20.

we are propelled forward in hope as our earthly celebration already participates in the future glory that will one day be ours.

LOOKING FORWARD

In the great chapter of Hebrews 11, the author sets before us many examples of faith from the Old Testament to encourage Christians in their lives of faith. Although the guiding word in that chapter is faith, it is faith defined in a way very closely connected to hope: "Now faith is the assurance of things hoped for, the conviction of things not seen" (Hebrews 11:1). The chief example is Abraham, who "was looking forward to the city that has foundations, whose designer and builder is God" (Hebrews 11:10). Yet Abraham was one of many of whom the author says,

> **These all died in faith, not having received the things promised, but having *seen them and greeted them from afar*, and having acknowledged that they were strangers and exiles on the earth. For people who speak thus make it clear that they are seeking a homeland. If they had been thinking of that land from which they had gone out, they would have had opportunity to return. But as it is, they desire a better country, that is, a heavenly one. Therefore God is not ashamed to be called their God, for He has prepared for them a city. (Hebrews 11:13–16, emphasis added)**

As Christians today, we take our place in that long line of people of faith, the great cloud of witnesses, and we look forward in hope to the future God promises. We confess with Christians of all times and places: "[We] look for the resurrection of the dead and the life of the world to come."

Reflection Questions

1. In your experience, do Christians in our time focus too much or too little on the "last things"?

2. How have you found funeral practices have changed during your lifetime, for better or worse?

3. How does our Christian hope encourage you in times of suffering?

4. What hymns to do with the last things are important to you?

5. How might the eschatological dimension of the Lord's Supper enrich your understanding and experience of it?

CONCLUSION

The hearing ear and the seeing eye,
the LORD has made them both.

PROVERBS 20:12

I envisage this book as a tapestry, where a number of different threads have been woven together. The first is a thread of cultural analysis. Christian truth does not change, yet we are called to confess it anew in every age. We do well, then, to be aware of the time and place in which God has placed us. The influences and emphases in the wider culture vary from age to age, and these have an impact on how Christians speak, act, think, and feel. So, this has been an attempt to think about how we live as Christians *today.* I've drawn especially on the work of Charles Taylor, who investigates and describes the way people in the West understand the world and themselves. I've found his insights very helpful, particularly the concepts of the immanent frame and expressive individualism.

The second thread is Luther's theology of the two kinds of righteousness, which I understand to go hand in hand with his articulation of the two realms and emphasis on faith and love. Even with the breadth of Luther's thought, he used various paradigms, turns of phrase, and other focused ways of writing and speaking that get at fundamental truths in memorable ways. The two kinds of righteousness are one such paradigm. It keeps clear the Gospel truth that we only ever stand confidently before God on the basis of Christ's finished work for us and that we passively receive that righteousness as a gift from outside ourselves by faith. It also then enables the discussion of the Christian person's responsibility of love in this life. I have found Robert Kolb's work especially helpful in how he identifies the two kinds of righteousness as Luther's way of speaking about what makes a person truly human. In an age of expressive individualism, the two kinds of righteousness paradigm points to the true life God intends outside of ourselves, rightly related to the Creator and His creation.

A third thread is my concept of the spirituality of looking, inspired by the final line of the Nicene Creed. For many years, I pondered this change of verb in the Creed as I confessed it Sunday by Sunday—the change from *believe* to *look*. I've also long been captivated by the many and varied images we are given in the New Testament for the Christian life. It seems to me that looking functions as one of these images or metaphors, although it also has a literal sense. This led me to wonder whether a book speaking about the shape of the Christian life could be written around this image. I ended up with the idea of looking up and looking out as being at the center, while further developing how we look up in faith and thanksgiving, look out and around in love to both Christians and non-Christians, rightly look in through self-examination, and look forward in hope.

A fourth thread is my own experience as a pastor in the Lutheran Church these past fifteen years or so. I've learned so much through the privilege of being invited into people's sins and struggles, their joys and encouragements. I've watched the ways people have endeavored to be faithful in their particular time and place with the cultural pressures that are on them. I've noted what seemed beneficial to them in all this as I preach, teach, listen, pray, forgive, bless, visit, and counsel. As helpful as the high-level cultural analysis is, it must go together with real, incarnate, concrete life with actual people. Each community I've served has had its own particularities, and it's both the joy and burden of a pastor to take the time to get to know these and minister accordingly.

A fifth and final thread is that of the Scriptures. In all I've written, whether picking up on the insights of others or developing my own ideas, I've endeavored to test these against the biblical text and let God's Word guide everything. At times, parts of the book were directly prompted by meditation on specific texts of Scripture. At others, an idea, event, or habit sent me back to the Bible to discern how we can understand it in the light of God's revealed truth. The main theme of the book—looking—originally sprang from the Creed. Yet it was fascinating for me to then go back to the Scriptures and discover the multifaceted and layered ways the Bible speaks about looking, seeing, and vision in relation to the life of faith. In this, I really only scratched the surface.

I wrote this book especially with Christian laypeople in mind, as a means of providing some encouragement in navigating and living the life of faith in these confusing and disorienting times. Perhaps some groups of Christians will find it helpful to read together and reflect via the discussion questions, and no doubt that experience will bring into focus the specific challenges and opportunities of the community into which God has placed them. I certainly hope that the book could lead people back to the ultimate source of truth and guidance in God's Word and back into reading Luther and the Lutheran Confessions.

As a pastor myself, I'm also aware that books like these can be helpful for the busy parish pastor to glean something from for their own work. Biblical commentaries have been essential to me over the years, but I've also benefited from other books that are already seeking, in some sense, to connect the biblical texts to the lives of the hearers and readers. Perhaps pastors, teachers, deaconesses, and other church workers may find something that gives them a little prompt or illustration for their next sermon, Bible study, or lesson.

Although people who are not yet believers have not been my primary audience, it would be a particular joy if those who are seeking, asking questions, and considering the Christian faith were to find something helpful here. It's been one of the highlights of my ministry to be able to work with these sorts of people and to participate in adults being baptized, confessing the faith, and joining in the life of the church. If the perspective I've offered here on what it is to be a Christian in today's world is valuable for them, thanks be to God.

I finish with two biblical texts that touch on the theme of looking and seeing that draw together many of the threads in these pages and continue to encourage me in my own life of looking up in faith and looking out in love:

> **After this I looked, and behold, a great multitude that no one could number, from every nation, from all tribes and peoples and languages, standing before the throne and before the Lamb, clothed in white robes, with palm branches in their hands, and crying out with a loud voice,**

"Salvation belongs to our God who sits on the throne, and to the Lamb!" (Revelation 7:9–10)

[Jesus says,] "Blessed are the pure in heart, for they shall see God." (Matthew 5:8)

SCRIPTURE INDEX

Old Testament

Genesis

1:27 44
2:18 8
3:8 40
3:9 8

Numbers

21:9 60

Deuteronomy

7:7–8 59–60
8:10–11 79

Psalms

13:2 29
23:5–6 152
25:7 90–91
42:5–6 .... 29, 30
106:1 77
136:1 87
139:7–8 41
145:15–16 82

Proverbs

4:25 119
13:20 119
20:12 155

Isaiah

25:6–9 152

Jeremiah

17:9 .... 21, 30, 35

Lamentations

3:40 134

New Testament

Matthew

5:8 159
5:13–14 95
5:29–30 125
5:43–45 116
6 130–31
6:25–34 112
7:3–5 .... 122, 133
7:11 77
11:3 141
14:19 .... 73, 81
19:28 139
22:37–40 41
24:27 143
24:42–44 12
24:50 141
28:20 64

Mark

6:34 109
7:21–23 .... 32, 35

Luke

2:19 29
2:25 140
2:38 140
10:29 109
10:33 105
10:34 109
13:11 33
14:12–14 100
17:17 79
21:28 69
21:34 139
22:17, 19 83
22:29–30 152
23:51 141

John

3:14–15 60
4:35 .... 12, 114
6:40 .... 57, 61
11:25–26 147
12:32–33 61
13:34 92
14:3 141
17:14–18 106
19:36, 37 61
20:29 12

Acts

1:11 .... 138, 141
16:15 99
16:40 99

Romans

3–4 62
3:21–26 62–63
4:25 7
6:1–13 7
7:15 31
7:21 35
8:13 125
10:17 12
12:1–2 118
12:9, 13 98–99

1 Corinthians

1:4 86
4 86
6 86
7:24 111
9:25–27 130
11 86
11:26 151
11:27–28 131
12 .... 96, 107
13 96
13:13 144
14 86

2 Corinthians

4:18 12
4:17–19 148
5:7 12
11 86
11:28 85

Galatians

3:27–28 64
5:6 49
6:2 .... 103, 104
6:10 92

Ephesians

1:15–16 37
1:18 12
2:8–9 95
4:4 95
5:15–16 121
5:25–26 95

Philippians

2:4 .... 89, 96
3:20 119
4:6 85

Colossians

1:3–5 144–45
1:4 49
1:9, 11–14 78
2–3 7
3:5 124
3:9–10 124
3:16 151

3:17 84

1 Timothy

6:12–14 41

Titus

2:13 141

Hebrews

6:19 145
11:1 153
11:10 .... 137, 153
11:13–16 153
11:16 151
12:1–2 70
12:2 12

James

1:5 119
1:17 76

1 Peter

2:10 95
4:8, 9 99

2 Peter

3:10–15 142

1 John

2:9–10 93
3:2 149
3:23 49

Jude

21 141

Revelation

7:9–10 159
19:6–9 152
22:20 152